The Critical Idiom
General Editor: JOHN D. JUMP

5   *The Absurd*

The Absurd / *Arnold P. Hinchliffe*

Methuen & Co Ltd

First published 1969
by Methuen & Co Ltd 11 New Fetter Lane London EC4
©1969 Arnold P. Hinchliffe
Printed in Great Britain
by Cox & Wyman Ltd, Fakenham, Norfolk

SBN 416 14530 2 Hardback
SBN 416 14540 X Paperback

Distributed in the U.S.A.
by Barnes & Noble Inc.

Contents

General Editor's Preface

This volume is one of a series of short studies, each dealing with a single key item, or a group of two or three key items, in our critical vocabulary. The purpose of the series differs from that served by the standard glossaries of literary terms. Many terms are adequately defined for the needs of students by the brief entries in these glossaries, and such terms will not be the subjects of studies in the present series. But there are other terms which cannot be made familiar by means of compact definitions. Students need to grow accustomed to them through simple and straightforward but reasonably full discussions of them. The purpose of this series is to provide such discussions.

Some of the terms in question refer to literary movements (e.g. 'Romanticism', 'Aestheticism', etc.), others to literary kinds (e.g. 'Comedy', 'Epic', etc.), and still others to stylistic features (e.g. 'Irony', 'The Conceit', etc.). Because of this diversity of subject-matter, no attempt has been made to impose a uniform pattern upon the studies. But all authors have tried to provide as full illustrative quotation as possible, to make reference whenever appropriate to more than one literature, and to compose their studies in such a way as to guide readers towards the short bibliographies in which they have made suggestions for further reading.

John D. Jump

University of Manchester

Preface

When it was first suggested to me that I should write a short account of *The Absurd*, my reaction was that Martin Esslin had already done it. It is his book which, more than anything else, has made the term and the philosophy widely available although restricted, unintentionally, to a small body of plays. These plays still strike me as the *most significant* literature of Absurdity but they have precedents and parallels elsewhere. Indeed, when the subject began to emerge as a document and not a slogan, the difficulty was to know where to begin and where to end.

I have taken it as axiomatic that for Absurdity to exist, God must be dead and that following this awareness there must be no attempt to substitute a transcendent *Alter Ego*. If, in the last analysis, writers produce as the great truth something which strikes us as very familiar – such as love or manly fellowship – those virtues now exist in a God-less context, and their achievement is the more difficult. The death of God and Transcendence safely eliminates most of the distinguished predecessors – such as Kafka or Dostoevsky – and limits the area of historical description to the last forty years. Even so, it proved impossible to cover, in the space available, either the novel or, more importantly, the philosophical background to the literature. But, as I have said, the play is *by its form* the best approach to *Absurdity* absurdly expressed – with one or two exceptions – and, therefore, no apology is needed for following in Martin Esslin's footsteps.

In *The Playwright as Thinker* (p. 127), Eric Bentley reminds us that critical terms can never be more than 'approximations and conveniences' and that when they become battlegrounds, 'when someone wants to know which of the varieties is the *real* thing, we have tumbled from rational discourse into superstition.' I have tried to avoid this error.

Arnold P. Hinchliffe

Acknowledgements

I should like to thank my colleague and editor, Professor J. D. Jump, for his unfailing assistance and kindness, and John Davidson for coping with the problems of typing the final version. The following permissions to quote from published works are acknowledged:

From *Experimental Drama*, edited by W. A. Armstrong, from the preface by W. A. Armstrong. Copyright © 1963 by G. Bell and Sons, Ltd.

From *The Theatre and Its Double* by Antonin Artaud (translated from the French by Mary Caroline Richards). Copyright © 1958 by Grove Press, Inc., and Calder and Boyars, Ltd. *The Theatre and Its Double* is to appear in Vol. 4 of *The Collected Works of Antonin Artaud*, in a new translation.

From *The Playwright as Thinker*, by Eric Bentley. Copyright © 1946 by Eric Bentley, by permission of the publishers, Harcourt, Brace and World, Inc.

From *The Messingkang Dialogues*, by Bertolt Brecht, translated by John Willett, by permission of Hope heresche and Steele.

From *Modern British Dramatists: A Collection of Critical Essays*, edited by John Russell Brown. Copyright © 1968. Reprinted by permission of Prentice-Hall, Inc., Englewood Cliffs, New Jersey, U.S.A.

From *The Theatre of Revolt* by Robert Brustein, by permission of Little, Brown & Co.

From *The Outsider* by Albert Camus, by permission of Hamish Hamilton, London and *The Stranger* by Albert Camus, Copyright © 1946 by Alfred A. Knopf, New York.

From *Beckett*, Writers and Critics Series, by R. N. Coe, by permission of the publishers, Oliver & Boyd, Ltd., Edinburgh.

From *The Vision of Jean Genet* by R. N. Coe. Copyright © R. N. Coe, 1968, by permission of the publishers, Peter Owen, Ltd., London and Grove Press, Inc., New York.

From *The Theatre of the Absurd* by Martin Esslin. Copyright © 1961 by Martin Esslin. Reprinted by permission of the publishers, Doubleday & Company, Inc., Eyre and Spottiswoode, Ltd., and Curtis Brown, Ltd., London.

From *Absurd Drama*, introduction by Martin Esslin, by permission of Penguin Books, Ltd.

From *Samuel Beckett: A Collection of Critical Essays*, edited by Martin Esslin. Copyright © 1965. Reprinted by permission of Prentice-Hall, Inc., Englewood Cliffs, New Jersey, U.S.A.

From *The Absurd Hero in American Fiction*, by David Galloway, by permission of the University of Texas Press.

From *Modern French Theatre* by Jacques Guicharnaud. Reprinted by permission of Yale University Press.

From *Victims of Duty* by Eugene Ionesco. *Three Plays* by Eugene Ionesco, translated by Donald Watson. Copyright © John Calder (Publishers) Ltd., 1958. Reprinted by permission of the publishers and Grove Press, Inc., New York.

From *The Modern American Theater: A Collection of Critical Essays*, edited by Alvin B. Kernan. Copyright © 1967. Reprinted by permission of Prentice-Hall, Inc., Englewood Cliffs, New Jersey, U.S.A.

From 'The Kitchen Sink', by G. Wilson Knight, in *Encounter* (December, 1963), by permission of the editor.

From *The Picaresque Saint* by R. W. B. Lewis. Reprinted by permission of Victor Gollancz Ltd., A. M. Heath & Co., Ltd., London, and J. B. Lippincott Company, New York.

From 'Notes on the Theatre of Cruelty', by Charles Marowitz, first published in *The Tulane Drama Review*, Vol. 11, No. 2 (T34) Winter, 1966. Copyright © 1966 *The Tulane Drama Review*;

copyright © 1967 *The Drama Review*. Reprinted by permission. All rights reserved.

From *The Writer and Commitment* by John Mander. Reprinted by permission of the publishers, Martin Secker & Warburg, Ltd., London.

From *Sartre* by Iris Murdoch: *Studies in Modern European Literature and Thought*. Reprinted by permission of Bowes and Bowes, London.

From *Eugene Ionesco*, Columbia Essays on Modern Writers, by L. C. Pronko. Reprinted by permission of Columbia University Press, New York.

From *Avant-Garde* by L. C. Pronko. Reprinted by permission of the University of California Press.

From 'Richard's Himself Again', by Gordon Rogoff, first published in *The Tulane Drama Review*, Vol. 11, No. 2 (T34) Winter, 1966. Copyright © 1966 *The Tulane Drama Review*; copyright 1967 *The Drama Review*. Reprinted by permission. All rights reserved.

From *Nausea* by Jean-Paul Sartre. Reprinted by permission of Hamish Hamilton, Ltd., London and New Directions Publishing Corporation, New York, publishers of Jean-Paul Sartre's *Nausea*; © 1964 by New Directions Publishing Corporation. All rights reserved.

From *What is Literature?* by Jean-Paul Sartre, translated from the French by Bernard Frechtman. Reprinted by permission of the publishers, Methuen & Co., Ltd., and The Philosophical Library (Publishers), New York.

From *Saint Genet* by Jean-Paul Sartre, translated from the French by Bernard Frechtman. Reprinted by permission of the publishers, W. H. Allen & Co., Ltd., and George Braziller, Inc., New York.

From *The Dark Comedy* by J. L. Styan. Copyright © 1962 by Cambridge University Press.

From *The Penguin Dictionary of the Theatre* by John Russell Taylor, reprinted by permission of Penguin Books, Ltd.

From *Tynan on Theatre* by Kenneth Tynan. Reprinted by permission of the publishers of *Curtains*, Longmans, Green & Co., Ltd.

From *The Philosophy of Sartre* by Mary Warnock. Reprinted by permission of the publishers, Hutchinson Publishing Group, Ltd., and Barnes & Noble, Inc., New York.

At the centre of European man, dominating the great moments of his life, there lies an essential absurdity.

ANDRÉ MALRAUX

What irks one most about the Absurdists is their pervasive tone of privileged despair.

KENNETH TYNAN

I

Critical Terms

The Shorter Oxford Dictionary (1965) defines 'absurd' as follows:

Absurd: 1. *Mus.* Inharmonious. 1617.
     2. Out of harmony with reason or propriety; in mod. use, plainly opposed to reason, and *hence* ridiculous, silly. 1557.

In *The Penguin Dictionary of Theatre* (1966) John Russell Taylor writes:

Absurd, Theatre of the. Term applied to a group of dramatists in the 1950s who did not regard themselves as a school but who all seemed to share certain attitudes towards the predicament of man in the universe: essentially those summarized by ALBERT CAMUS in his essay *The Myth of Sisyphus* (1942). This diagnoses humanity's plight as purposelessness in an existence out of harmony with its surroundings (absurd literally means out of harmony). Awareness of this lack of purpose in all we do . . . produces a state of metaphysical anguish which is the central theme of the writers in the Theatre of the Absurd, most notably SAMUEL BECKETT, EUGÈNE IONESCO, ARTHUR ADAMOV, JEAN GENET, and HAROLD PINTER. What distinguishes these and other, lesser figures (ROBERT PINGET, N. F. SIMPSON, EDWARD ALBEE, FERNANDO ARRABAL, GÜNTER GRASS) from earlier dramatists who have mirrored a similar concern in their work is that the ideas are allowed to shape the form as well as the content: all semblance of logical construction, of the rational linking of idea with idea in an intellectually viable argument, is abandoned, and instead the irrationality of experience is transferred to the stage. The procedure has both its advantages and its limitations. Most dramatists of the absurd have found it difficult to sustain a whole evening in the theatre without compromising somewhat . . . Indeed, by 1962 the movement seemed to have spent its force, though as a liberating influence on the conventional theatre its effects continue to be felt.

This particular application of a current philosophical term to drama was the invention of Martin Esslin in his book *The Theatre of the Absurd* (1961) and, since this book more than anything else has made the term familiar to the English reading public, it seems reasonable to begin a discussion of *Absurdity* in this context. It has, in fact, become an embarrassingly successful catch-phrase (as Esslin ruefully admits in his introduction to the anthology of plays published by Penguin under the title *Absurd Drama*, 1965), but frequently convenience can be allowed to outweigh adequacy in a critical formulation. We can, then, conveniently describe drama in England as recently falling under three headings: first, Poetic, followed by two apparently opposed movements, Angry and Absurd, the fusion of which leads to innumerable sub-divisions so that, by 1968, John Russell Brown, editing a series of essays on Modern British Theatre and Dramatists, could write in an introduction:

> The new plays have been given all sorts of labels: 'kitchen-sink drama' was one of the first; neo-realist; drama of non-communication; absurd drama; comedy of menace; dark comedy; drama of cruelty. But no cap has fitted for more than a year or two; none has been big enough for more than one or two heads; and often the caps seem more suitable for the journalists who invent them than for the dramatists on whom they are thrust. Perhaps the first thing to say about the new dramatists is that they keep the critics on the run.
>
> (*Modern British Dramatists*, p. 2)

And, one might add, audiences too, for going to the theatre nowadays is a hazardous occupation. There is a conspicuous lack of a prevailing form so that neither critic nor audience can assume what shape the play will take. If this is confusing for critics (and often shocking for audiences) it does suggest that, as W. A. Armstrong puts it, playwrights 'have made the theatre a rallying-point in the perennial struggle of the human imagination against religious complacency, moral apathy, and social conformity' (Preface, *Experimental Drama*, London, 1963, p. 9).

The poetic drama would seem to have been dead before either Angry or Absurd dramas reached the stage. Its history is explored by Denis Donoghue in *The Third Voice* (Princeton, 1959) and he is probably correct in suggesting that poets who come to the theatre are often loath to concede that words are not enough to carry the burden of drama (p. 249). But we should not write off the experiment too casually: without 'poetic' plays – the work of Eliot and Fry, for example – the subsequent plays of Anger and Absurdity, both of which rely on language enormously, might not have been possible or as successful.

Of the two succeeding labels, Angry and Absurd, it was the Angry Drama which made the more immediate impact on the English theatre, so much so that John Russell Taylor, in *Anger and After* (1962), effectively dates his contemporary period from the first performance of *Look Back in Anger* at the Royal Court Theatre on 8 May 1956. The more European-based drama which we call Absurd took longer to percolate into our theatrical experience, but when it did it was ultimately recognized as fulfilling the obsenite maxim of 'poetic creation in the plain unvarnished speech of reality' (Kenneth Muir, *Contemporary Theatre*, p. 113) and is frequently discussed, by Esslin and others, in terms of 'poetic', just as, in retrospect, the tirades of Jimmy Porter strike us as more important for the manner of saying than for what has been said. Indeed, in retrospect, the success of *Look Back in Anger* is, as Gordon Rogoff remarks, a cause of wonder:

By what was undoubtedly sleight-of-thought, the play gave all the appearances of being lined up squarely with New Left political positions. It *seemed* to be about commitment, it *seemed* to be a protest, it *seemed* to be political, and it even *seemed* to be new, though the only startling formal 'innovation' was that what *seemed* to be a five-character play was really a monologue.

('Richard's Himself Again', TDR, 1966, pp. 30–1)

B

The division between Anger and Absurd, between, we mig[
say, Brecht and Ionesco, was summed up by Kenneth Tyna[
where Ionesco says misery is constant Brecht would argue tha
some kinds of misery are curable, and after they have been cure[
there will be time to look at the universal ones (*Tynan on Theatr[
Penguin, 1964, pp. 188–91). *Committed* literature is itself a vexe[
question. John Mander in his study of the subject, *The Writer an[
Commitment* (London, 1961) points out that *Look Back in Ang[
was a vehement play but it was also non-committal, and that i[
any case commitment cannot merely mean political engagemen[
Any writer is committed in the sense that his writing seeks valu[
in a valueless world: 'Commitment is universal: the poet of sul[
jectivity chooses to explore its inner rather than outer face' ([
180–1). Our most committed dramatist is probably Arnold Weske[
yet his solution is decidedly that of an artist rather than a morali[
or propagandist: namely, that reform can be achieved throug[
education and art. If we were to agree that generally Angry Theat[
is topical, particular, and political, whereas Absurd Theatre is tim[
less, universal, and philosophical, we should then have to accou[
for Theatre of Cruelty which is angry in intention and absurd i[
impression! We should also have to answer Martin Esslin's co[
tention in an essay on Harold Pinter that Absurd Theatre conce[
trating as it does on a basic situation is as relevant socially as pla[
by social realists, and, since it does not reflect merely topical pr[
occupations, more enduring because it is unaffected by the fluctua[
tions of political and social circumstances ('Pinter and the Absurd[
Twentieth Century (1961), 169, No. 1008, p. 185). *Quot homines, t[
sententiae.*

Nor is the form the plays take helpful in maintaining the usef[
separateness of our critical terms. The theories of Bertolt Brec[
which underpin Committed Drama stem from the two produce[
who dominated the stage when Brecht was young, Reinhardt an[
Piscator, who both laid special emphasis on the participation [

e audience in events on the stage. Piscator, in particular, aimed
t making a performance in the theatre a demonstration of work-
g-class solidarity (see Ronald Gray, *Brecht*, London, 1961,
Chapter 4). From this Brecht formulated his famous A-effect
(sometimes called the V or E-effect) which he claims is an artistic
echnique of great antiquity:

> To achieve the A-effect the actor must give up his *complete conversion*
> into the stage character. He *shows* the character, he *quotes* his lines, he
> *repeats* a real-life incident. The audience is not entirely 'carried away';
> it need not conform psychologically, adopt a fatalistic attitude towards
> fate as portrayed. (It can feel anger where the character feels joy, and
> so on. It is free, and sometimes even encouraged, to imagine a
> different course of events or to try and find one, and so forth.) The
> incidents are *historicised* and socially *set*.
>
> (*The Messingkauf Dialogues*, trans.
> John Willett, London, 1965, p. 104)

Such a theatre is, apparently, antagonistic to empathy (though
he audience can and does resist this antagonism with remarkable
uccess, as when they make Mother Courage the heroine of the
lay of that name, and not the villain); it does not seek to intoxi-
ate, supply with illusions, and make the spectator forget the world
r reconcile himself to its injuries. But, whereas we can and often
o sympathize with Brecht's characters, in Absurd Drama it is
lore difficult, for there we have characters whose motives are
idden and whose actions we cannot understand, and thus,
onically, Esslin is once more plausible when he suggests that the
-effect happens in *Absurd Drama* more completely than in
Brecht's own plays.

It is better not to push the genres too far apart. Brechtian tech-
iques of song and dance bring to socially committed plays an
tmosphere of absurdity. It has been argued that John Arden,
robably the most complete Brechtian in British Theatre, is not
nconnected with Absurd practices (J. D. Hainsworth, 'John

Arden and the Absurd', *A Review of English Literature*, Vol. 7 No. 4 (Oct. 1966), pp. 42–9) and David J. Grossvogel in *Four Playwrights and a Postscript* (1962) finds no difficulty in linking together Brecht, Ionesco, Beckett, and Genet as angry dramatists whose anger is directed as much at the corruptness of the stage as at the corruptness of the world reflected on the stage. If we look at the work of Peter Hall and Peter Brook at Stratford and the Aldwych we shall recognize, in productions of such widely divergent plays as the *Marat-Sade*, *Henry VI*, and *King Lear*, a single image: it is that the world is an existential nightmare from which reason, forgiveness, and hope are absent: a place less to live in than to endure (Rogoff, 'Richard's Himself Again', *Tulane Drama Review* 34 (1966), p. 37). We shall also note that what John Russell Taylor calls 'a situation patently rigged for anger' is another form of the Absurdist's 'extreme situation'.

Nor should we be disturbed overmuch by the ephemeral nature of drama. The theatre is always in trouble because, as Eric Bentley puts it, its success depends upon 'too rare a set of coincidences':

> A poem needs performer and listener. Closer to drama is the symphony, which requires teamwork, co-ordination at the hands of a conductor, a large audience, and a heap of money. The drama, however, boasting of being a meeting place of all the arts, requires a too rare conjunction of economic, social, and artistic elements. Especially in its synthetic manifestations, which include everything in musical-choreographic-spectacular-mimetic-rhetorical theater from the Greeks to *Tannhäuser* and beyond, drama is the most impossible of the arts.
>
> (*The Playwright as Thinker*, p. 233)

Ten years is good going in an impossible art.

In *New English Dramatists 12* (1968) Irving Wardle writes of a body of work known as the theatre of the absurd:

> Its characteristics are: the substitution of an inner landscape for the outer world; the lack of any clear division between fantasy and fact;

a free attitude towards time, which can expand or contract according to subjective requirements; a fluid environment which projects mental conditions in the form of visual metaphors; and an iron precision of language and construction as the writer's only defence against the chaos of living experience.

That Mr Wardle can write that definition so easily is because seven years earlier Esslin wrote a book called *The Theatre of the Absurd.*

2
The Theatre of the Absurd

Martin Esslin's authoritative survey of this kind of drama was published in 1961 (and in England in 1962) and it did not escape criticism. The scepticism of Kenneth Tynan illustrates a very reasonable disquiet:

> Tracing the forebears of the Absurd, Mr Esslin leads us back to the mime plays of antiquity; to the Commedia dell'Arte; to Edward Lear and Lewis Carroll; to Jarry, Strindberg, and the young, Rimbaud-impregnated Brecht; to the Dadaists and Tristan Tzara (who called one of his plays 'the biggest swindle of the century in three acts'); to the Surrealists and Antonin Artaud's *Theatre of Cruelty*; to Kafka, and to Joyce.
>
> All this is helpful and credible. But when Mr Esslin ropes in Shakespeare, Goethe, and Ibsen as harbingers of the Absurd, one begins to feel that the whole history of dramatic literature has been nothing but a prelude to the glorious emergence of Beckett and Ionesco. Overstatement and Mr Esslin are not strangers, as may be guessed from the fact that he calls N. F. Simpson 'a more powerful social critic than any of the social realists'; and I wish I had an extra month of life for every playwright in connexion with whose work Mr Esslin refers to 'the human condition'.
>
> (*Tynan on Theatre*, p. 190.)

When Esslin wrote the introduction to a Penguin anthology of plays called *Absurd Drama* (1965) he lamented the success of his title – a catch-phrase much used and much abused – but he still felt that it could prove useful as 'a kind of intellectual shorthand for a complex pattern of similarities in approach . . . of shared philosophical and artistic premises.' Such a label is useful not as 'a binding classification' but to help us gain insight into a work of art (cf. *Absurd Drama*, pp. 7–9). Once defined and understood, such a term helps us to evaluate works of previous epochs and he gives as an example (which not everyone will find felicitous) the work of Jan Kott on Shakespeare which produced Peter Brook's *King Lear* influenced by Beckett's *Endgame*.

This claim of usefulness which Esslin presumably took for granted in 1961 is echoed in the revised version of *The Theatre of the Absurd* (Pelican, 1968). The revision and enlargement are mainly a matter of bringing the work up to date (including the excellent bibliography) with the addition of a short eighth chapter called 'Beyond the Absurd'. In his preface to this edition Esslin comments on the speed with which yesterday's incomprehensible play has become today's classic, and the success, in many ways unfortunate, of his own book – or at least the title. He repeats that there is no such thing as a movement of Absurd dramatists; the term is useful – 'a device to make certain fundamental traits which seem to be present in the works of a number of dramatists accessible to discussion by tracing features they have in common' (*The Theatre of the Absurd*, p. 10). It is, he argues, only by a 'profound misunderstanding' that it has come to be regarded as anything more. It may be that Esslin's enthusiasm was partly to blame for such a misunderstanding, but the record must now be considered as straight. Esslin has written a crucial book on a group of plays which incorporate certain beliefs and use certain methods and which, briefly, we call Absurd Drama.

By far the most surprising thing about these plays is that in spite of breaking all the rules they are successful:

If a good play must have a cleverly constructed story, these have no story or plot to speak of; if a good play is judged by subtlety of characterization and motivation, these are often without recognizable characters and present the audience with almost mechanical puppets; if a good play has to have a fully explained theme, which is neatly exposed and finally solved, these often have neither a beginning nor an end; if a good play is to hold the mirror up to nature and portray the manners and mannerisms of the age in finely observed sketches, these seem often to be reflections of dreams and nightmares; if a good play relies on witty repartee and pointed dialogue, these often consist of incoherent babblings.

(The Theatre of the Absurd, pp. 21–2)

This kind of play springs, Esslin suggests, from the disillusionment and loss of certitude characteristic of our times and reflected in works like *The Myth of Sisyphus* (1942) by Camus – where the word *Absurd* appears – and in the plays of his four major dramatists, Beckett, Adamov, Ionesco, and Genet. The senselessness of life and loss of ideals had, of course, been reflected in dramatists like Giraudoux, Anouilh, Sartre, and Camus, but whereas they had presented irrationality in terms of the old conventions, dramatists in the Theatre of the Absurd sought a more appropriate form. They do not argue about absurdity, they 'present it in being' (*The Theatre of the Absurd*, p. 25). Like the Poetic Theatre, Absurd Theatre relies heavily on dream and fantasy but, unlike that theatre, it rejects consciously 'poetic' dialogue in favour of the banal. Although centred on Paris it is distinctly international in flavour, as is emphasized by the four leading exponents chosen by Esslin: the Irish Beckett, the Russian Adamov, the Rumanian Ionesco – who choose to be Parisians; and the Frenchman Genet. These dramatists are followed by about eighteen contemporary playwrights of whom Pinter and Simpson are the British representatives. All these dramatists partake, in one form or another, of the 'Tradition of the Absurd' which, in Chapter 6, proves to be very far-flung indeed, incorporating devices from the circus, mimes, clowning, verbal nonsense, and the literature of dream and fantasy which often has a strong allegorical component (Esslin, p. 318). An exciting chapter, it nevertheless seems so all-embracing that Tynan's scepticism seems justified. The tradition is more obviously pertinent when Esslin approaches the iconoclasts, Jarry, Apollinaire, and Dada. It comes as a surprise, however, to find the early Brecht in a list of Absurd dramatists. The conclusion Esslin reaches is in many ways disappointing. Having demonstrated that the Absurd Theatre is part of a rich and varied tradition, Esslin is required to show in what way it produces something really new, and he suggests that it is 'the unusual way in which various familiar attitudes of mind and literary idioms are interwoven' and the fact that this approach has met 'with a wide response from a broadly based public' which he admits is characteristic not so much of the Theatre of the Absurd as of the times (Esslin, p. 388).

Esslin's more important suggestions occur in a chapter called 'The Significance of the Absurd'. This analysis begins with a characteristic philosophical reference (Esslin was trained in Philosophy and English at Vienna University): that the number of people for whom God is dead has greatly increased since Nietzsche published *Also Sprach Zarathustra* in 1883. The Theatre of the Absurd is one of the ways of facing up to a universe that has lost its meaning and purpose. As such it fulfils a double role. Its first and more obvious role is satirical, when it criticizes a society that is petty and dishonest. Its second and more positive aspect is shown when it faces up to Absurdity in plays where man is 'stripped of the accidental circumstances of social position or historical context, confronted with basic choices, the basic situations of his existence' (Esslin, p. 391).

Such a theatre is involved in the relatively few problems that remain: life, death, isolation, and communication, and it can, by its nature, only communicate 'one poet's most intimate and personal intuition of the human situation, his own sense of being, his individual vision of the world' (Esslin, pp. 392–3). This vision receives a form which Esslin sees as analogous to a Symbolist or Imagist poem in which, however, language is only one component, and not necessarily the dominant one. For language has suffered its own devaluation, a fact which Esslin sees as very contemporary from the point of view of either the philosopher, Wittgenstein, or the mass media.

The resulting play, ironically, produces the effect desired by Brecht from his didactic Socialist theatre: alienation. We find it very difficult to identify with characters in Absurd drama (thus, though their situation is often painful and violent, the audience can laugh at them): but, where Brecht hoped to 'activate the audience's critical, intellectual attitude', Absurd drama speaks 'to a deeper level of the audience's mind' (Esslin, p. 402). It challenges the audience to make sense of non-sense, to face the situation consciously rather than feel it vaguely, and perceive, with laughter, the fundamental absurdity.

Given such a drama, what criteria can be applied to assess the quality of such works in the theatre? Esslin lists these as 'invention, the complexity of the poetic images invoked, and the skill with which they are combined and sustained' and, even more importantly, 'the *reality* and *truth* of the vision these images embody' (p 412). The italics are Esslin's and we could perhaps quarrel with the subjectivity and vagueness of such concepts for critical purposes.

Such a theatre, then, presents anxiety and despair, a sense of loss at the disappearance of solutions, illusions, and purposefulness. Facing up to this loss means that we face up to *reality itself* (italics mine); thus Absurd drama becomes a kind of modern mystical experience which Esslin compares to the recent fashion for Zen Buddhism (a system that also bases itself on the rejection of conceptual thought):

> Today, when death and old age are increasingly concealed behind euphemisms and comforting baby talk, and life is threatened with being smothered in the mass consumption of hypnotic mechanized vulgarity, the need to confront man with the *reality* of his situation is greater than ever. For the dignity of man lies in his ability to face

reality in all its senselessness; to accept it freely, without fear, without illusions – and to laugh at it.

(Esslin, p. 419)

The italics are, again, mine and exist to show that possibly language, even on Absurd Drama, tends to be as loose and question-begging as anywhere else.

In his last chapter, Esslin suggests that Absurd Drama has been absorbed, but still shows itself 'in the manifold strivings of a Protean *avant-garde*'. Such a summary can only hint at the flavour of Esslin's important, lively, and provocative book; it commands respect and attention, and it suitably directs our attention to the philosophical basis of Absurdity.

3
First Outsiders

Esslin's appropriation of the term for theatre and its subsequent success is unfortunate in one way, namely, because it has obscured the widespread use of the word 'absurd' in other contexts. In 1956 Colin Wilson published a book called *The Outsider* which enjoyed considerable notoriety. Beginning with the anonymous hero of Henri Barbusse's novel *Hell*, he considers Sartre's novel *Nausea*, Camus and Hemingway. After pointing out that in previous societies the outsider had a place – as a romantic dreamer – he looks at Hermann Hesse and, surprisingly, Henry James, before turning to outsiders in real life (T. E. Lawrence, Van Gogh, and Nijinsky). He covers, in rapid succession, what Yeats called the 'tragic generation' of the nineteenth century, Count Axel, the vastations of Swedenborg, T. S. Eliot, Nietzsche, Dostoevsky (the outsider is in everything Dostoevsky wrote) and comes to the following conclusions: that the Outsider would like to cease being one, and wants to be balanced; he would like to understand the human soul and escape from triviality, and to do this he needs to know how to express himself, for that is the means by which he can know himself and his possibilities. Two discoveries emerge: that his salvation lies in extremes, and that the idea of a way out often comes in visions or moments of intensity (*The Outsider*, p. 202). For his visionaries Wilson chooses George Fox and William Blake, with Ramakrishna and Gurdjieff for good measure, and arrives at the idea that the individual who begins as an Outsider may finish as a saint.

The Outsider was the first of a series of books culminating in the sixth and last volume called *Beyond the Outsider* (1965) in which Wilson hoped to create a 'new existentialism' to replace what he calls the bankrupt article of Sartre and Heidegger. Like Esslin, Wilson casts his net wide, and the result is exciting if not always conclusive.

Our first important Outsider is in the work of André Malraux who suggested, in 1925, that *'at the centre of European man, dominating the great moments of his life, there lies an essential absurdity'*. The italics are Malraux's, not mine, and the phrase occurs in *La Tentation de l'occident*, published in 1926. Four years later, in 1930, he published a novel called *The Royal Way* in which, in the words of R. W. B. Lewis, Malraux 'surveyed the major motifs of a generation of fiction yet unwritten' jumbling them together in a short and rather overcrowded book (Lewis, *The Picaresque Saint*, p. 279).

The legend of Malraux has made biography difficult. He was noted, when young, for making trips to the Far East; he was a member of the Communist Party (but later supported de Gaulle); and he was involved in the Spanish Civil War. Thoroughly educated in art, archaeology, and anthropology, it was his search for Khmerian bas-reliefs that landed him in court in Pnompenh, where he was sentenced to three years in jail – an experence that Frohock feels was crucial to his subsequent development. Certainly humiliation in his novels is linked with prison, court, or interrogation: 'It gave him a first experience of humiliation, for which he could hold Europe – and European values – responsible. Hence the feeling of estrangement which, together with an awareness of the Absurd, characterizes the early novels' (Frohock, *André Malraux and the Tragic Imagination*, p. 12).

Whether this was so or not, the man who in 1920 could be regarded as a pure example of a surrealist writer began on his return to Europe in 1925 to write *The Temptation of the West* where Europe figures as a 'great cemetery'. Sixty-five pages long, the book consists of letters supposedly written between two young men: five by A.D. – a young European travelling in the East, and the rest by Ling W.-T., a young Chinese travelling in Europe. The more this young man sees of Europe the more convinced he becomes that European thought and culture are based on confusion and a wrong notion of reality, a conviction expressed in the famous phrase quoted above and used as an epigraph to this study. A.D. agrees that Western Man is a creature of the Absurd, and uses the rest of the book to provide added reasons, and warn that the disease is spreading to the Orient. Obviously, for A.D., it is not merely God who is dead, but man also: standing alone under an empty heaven without remedy.

Malraux is clearly interested in ideas, but he is not a philosopher, and therefore is less committed to the logic of discourse and more to a passionate, even poetic, presentation of ideas. In *The Voices of Silence* (1951) he has written a general survey of the decline of Christianity and the loss of absolutes in the Western world. Following such a loss, man confronts *le destin, l'absurde* and *l'angoisse*. 'Destiny' is Malraux's word for all we want to escape but cannot, and since all our actions are directed against the inevitable they are 'absurd'; because we sense this absurdity we experience 'anguish'. The opposition of East and West which we find in *The Temptation* is important here, for the Oriental man seeks to surrender to the irrational, but Western man, hopelessly committed to making sense of the world and life, cannot yield to the irrational. Given this condition, Malraux is one of the first to prescribe the consequence: action, the exercise of this new liberty. Fr Gannon, in his study of Malraux, conceded that Malraux and other contemporary writers may have written about this view of the world better than ever before but, he also remarks, there is a suspicion 'that they frequently prefer the saying of it all to the solving of it' (*The Honor of Being a Man*, p. 36). Malraux's response to destiny, which invariably means death, is far from nihilistic: it is a call to furious activity.

In *The Temptation* Malraux feared that the East would be contaminated by a European malaise, and two years later, in an essay called *A European Youth* (1927), he tackled the basic difficulty of Western man: individualism, and his inability to establish relationships with other individuals. The young men of Europe, he wrote, were searching for an idea, but, surprisingly, he does not mention Communism, nor for that matter any positive action. During the years 1925–30 there had been a great many 'ideas' embodied in the various 'isms' – modernism, futurism, cubism, dadaism, surrealism – but they had produced, ultimately, nothing but fuss. Then certain men – like Malraux – brought, in the words of Claude-Edmonde Magny, 'the basic questions into fashion' (quoted Frohock, p. 33). Possibly Malraux's experiences in the Orient made him ask these questions. His early novels are full of death, solitude, defeat, and suffering, with scarcely a hint that life could possibly acquire meaning through action and sacrifice, until *Man's Estate* in 1933. Even the condition of solitude is seen as a by-product of Absurdity: in *The Temptation* we are cut off *because* of an untenable notion of reality, and in *A European Youth* we are cut off *because* of the individualism inherent in our civilization. His first two novels suggest, however, that Absurdity is not a European disease, but rather a condition of humanity.

Both of these novels, *The Conquerors* and *The Royal Way*, share a basic fable (a man goes out East, meets another man whom he watches go through the ordeal of discovering his limitations as a human being), and a basic theme, Absurdity.

The Conquerors (1928), Malraux's first serious novel, is set in south-east Asia. Garine joins the Bolsheviks and comes to the Orient to support the revolution, working as a propaganda agent with Borodin, a member of the International. But it is obvious that Garine's actions are merely part of the battle against his sense of Absurdity, things go wrong, and the novel ends with plans for a trip to England for his health (though he knows that he is dying). Where did this awareness of Absurdity start? Brought to trial in

Switzerland for financing abortions, Garine had felt for the trial and its participants the disgust that follows recognition of Absurdity. Once he had perceived this, he was 'free' – he could act as he chose – but being partly a philosopher (and not, for example, a gangster) he could believe that the world was absurd, but his actions need not be. His participation in revolution looks like a solution. But the trial in Switzerland had convinced him that the world was absurd not evil (in which case it could be improved), and the revolution, therefore, merely provides an opportunity for action through which he escapes – aware of the Absurd without giving in to it. Trotsky, in his article on the novel, wrote that what Garine needed was a good dose of Marxism! (quoted Frohock, p. 44). But *The Conquerors* is a novel not a manifesto, and Malraux was trying to show man's fate, not the blue-print of a revolution. Garine involves himself in a revolution for, like all Malraux's heroes, he feels that blood, murder, torture, revolution and particularly death confer authenticity upon an action.

The technique helps us to feel the Absurdity. Malraux uses a first-person narrator who has known Garine a long time and virtually keeps a diary, using the present tense and writing down each happening as soon as it has taken place, without apparent knowledge of what will happen next. The style is impressionistic, rarely needing a complete grammatical sentence, but the scenes, observed with a good cinematographic eye, have a compelling accuracy. Such a style, while it distances the readers, renders characterization difficult, and the characters only gradually emerge as men.

Malraux described *The Conquerors* as 'an adolescent book' and omitted his second novel, *The Royal Way*, entirely from the Pléiade edition of his novels. Although *The Royal Way* (1930) contains no revolution, it has basically the same theme. Perken and Claude Vannec go into the jungles of Cambodia in search of Khmerian bas-reliefs. Like Garine, Perken is hostile to established values, haunted by death, exiled from society, while Vannec has left Europe because he shares this feeling. After the two men have found the sculptures, they press on into the jungle and come to a Moi village where they make friends with the natives, only to discover that another European, Grabot, is already there. Grabot, the one person whom Perken had really admired, has been blinded by the Moi and is held captive on a treadmill – a warning of what will happen to Perken and Vannec unless they can escape. But in escaping Perken falls on an upturned spear, the wound is infected and he dies anyway, as he had lived, alone. Like Garine, Perken uses action not to establish a new order, but to express rejection of the old.

With *Man's Estate* (1933) – another novel of the Chinese revolution – Malraux established himself as an important writer, and was awarded the Prix Goncourt. It is quintessential Malraux from the opening chapter, when Tchen meditates on whether to drive the knife through the mosquito net or raise it, to the final execution. For all its leading characters death, surrounded by terror, cruelty and torture, is the inevitable end. The initial act of violence confers upon Tchen his essential status in the world, and condemns him to a special kind of anguish, renewing his fundamental feeling of isolation and his old obsession with death. By this act Tchen is changed from the man who joined the revolution to lessen the sufferings of the poor into an outsider, fascinated by death. But he is the only hero in the book who forgets the cause of his dying. For the revolutionaries in this novel have goals or purposes that are definable, and if the Absurd is still dominant some characters repudiate its meaninglessness by joining a cause. Tchen is the last Malraux character to achieve freedom through death; the others – Kyo or Katow, for example – die for the ideal of the revolution as they see it and suggest the value expressed in Malraux's most famous phrase (from *The Voices of Silence*): the honour of being a man.

The use of revolution as a setting for this discovery presents certain difficulties, particularly when we consider the apparent inconsistency of Malraux's own political loyalties. In the 1930s writers felt very strongly the need to be committed: *l'engagement* – the choice each man must make, taking full responsibility for all the consequences. The Communist Party was a fairly popular choice. But Malraux's heroes make strange Communists (as Trotsky's comment on Garine shows). In fact, the discipline of the Communist Party is as irksome as that of religion to existential man, who must have total liberty; and, although Jean-Paul Sartre gets round this problem, it haunts most of Malraux's heroes.

Frohock finds the theme of Absurdity absent from *Days of Hope* (1937), but, as its title implies, Malraux is working out a possible answer. A long novel with many characters (none of whom is dominant), it is unified only by its theme: there is hope, belief in man when men fight together in a common cause. Manly fellowship in wartime clearly excludes loneliness (for example) but it is a response in an extreme situation, and is, therefore, of questionable value for those of us who do not have a revolution at hand. This should not be overlooked; revolution and brutal action are the devices by which Malraux arrives at comradeship, an answer to absurdity, but a very restricted one. The expression of the solution is, perhaps inevitably, less forceful than the description of the dilemma; it strikes us as a platitude, it demands special circumstances, and the activity must be furious, to blot out the sense of Absurdity, one suspects, rather than make sense of it. But Malraux's early heroes have much in common: intelligence and lucidity – as Frohock sardonically remarks, for characters who have trouble communicating with each other, they communicate remarkably well with the reader (Frohock, p. 142). They are all eaten by obsessions, lonely, refugees from the bourgeoisie moved into the strange world of war and revolution. Love is no answer. There is not one important woman character in Malraux's novels, and Fr Gannon can find only two cases of real love: each man must come to his own personal vision of life, and it is not a particularly happy one. Man's destiny is suffering and death – which he can defeat by affirming human dignity and participating in a sense of brotherhood with other men.

Since about 1947 Malraux appears to have returned to his interest in Art (see Gannon, Section iv), and it seems that his final answer is to send the honest or authentic man to Art, where he will be in the company of saints, sages, and heroes. It is in the early novels that we find the situation and the code, both of which bear a strong resemblance to the work of Malraux's contemporary, an expatriate American writer, Ernest Hemingway.

Hemingway was, from the beginning, also convinced that to live 'in our time' was somehow unusually difficult. John Killinger, in his study called *Hemingway and the Dead Gods* (1960) – appropriately subtitled 'A Study in Existentialism', reviews the background to Hemingway's work, such as the publication in 1927 of Heidegger's unreadable work *Sein und Zeit*, and later Camus and Sartre, and concludes that such a hard philosophy 'offering nothing but anguish and a tantalizing hunger for an authenticity that must be re-won moment by moment, challenging even in its severity, is especially forged to the temper of modern man' (Killinger, p. 13). Killinger has no intention of making Hemingway a poor man's Heidegger, but suggests that the novels are patterned in existentialist terms. Hemingway's heroes resemble other existential heroes in their insistence that only in the face of death can they achieve honesty. Hemingway's use of *nada* (for example, in the short story *A Clean Well-Lighted Place*) is similar to the idea of Nothing which we find in Heidegger and Sartre, and when the hero returns from war or hunting or the bullfight – all extreme situations which compel the moment of truth – Hemingway's distinction between the simple and the complicated life closely resembles Sartre's distinction between sincerity and bad faith. Hemingway's heroes, too, experience nausea (literally, in some cases), and the death of the gods leaves a moral anarchy which compels them to formulate a code: *pundonor* – 'the mysterious mixture of pride, dignity, defiance, and honour. It is a code for those who face death often and are not afraid' (Killinger, p. 79). And if by *The Old Man and the Sea* we find Christological imagery, Hemingway's Christ is very much a humanist. The only peace in our time must be strenuously achieved. In the 1930s Hemingway's characters, too, are politically involved, but Hemingway soon returns to the extreme situation of war or death which produces liberty. As in Malraux, women are excluded as far as possible, although this is more difficult since Hemingway's heroes are presented as extremely virile. But a woman, if sexually necessary, is a complication to the proper existence of man, which is to face death alone.

The novels of Hemingway, then, can be seen as essentially in the same vein as those of his colleague Malraux. Both insist on the extreme importance of the individual who seeks to be honest or authentic and accepts responsibility for that honesty, and both find that decision is best made when confronting death. Writers and philosophers connected with Absurdity are unanimous in rejecting suicide, and insisting on the importance of death, and we can best understand this by looking at Heidegger's conclusion. This was that of all human activities and experiences death was unique. Whereas we can think of other people being involved in activities such as writing a book or going on a holiday, death involves only the person dying. Tolstoy's *The Death of Ivan Ilyich* (1886) gives literary expression to this idea. By constantly facing death, rather than trying to forget its existence, the hero preserves his honesty.

Killinger expressly rejects the idea that Hemingway was an existentialist. As he points out, there is no known liaison between him and them; but a young expatriate American living in Paris at a certain crucial time might have imbibed something of the atmosphere. The similarities, which are striking, come most probably not from collaboration, but because thinking men might arrive at similar conclusions when placed in the same time and place. At this point it is useful to remember that Absurdity is not simply a French matter, although the French do appear to have felt more absurd than most, and our principal witnesses, after Malraux, are French. In chronological order they are Jean-Paul Sartre and Albert Camus.

4
Jean-Paul Sartre

The name of Jean-Paul Sartre is usually closely linked with 'existentialist', although the epithet was first applied by Gabriel Marcel and seized upon by French journalists as a convenient label. Sartre thought of himself as a phenomenologist (that is, one who studies the way consciousness perceives objects), but had resigned himself to using the word by 1946. Existentialism is dismissed by British philosophers with a shrug as an example of 'Continental excess and rankness', but it has been, in France, a storm-centre of violent controversies of both a religious and a political nature (John Passmore, *A Hundred Years of Philosophy*, Penguin 1968, p. 467, and p. 488). Certainly existentialists are open to the complaint that they dramatize the ordinary. Sensible people accept the contingency of the world and get on with the business of living in it, while existentialists cry out in anguish that they are gratuitous in an impossible world!

In fact, existentialism is a trend not a school. Walter Kaufmann, in his anthology *Existentialism from Dostoevsky to Sartre* (1956), admits that it is nothing more than a label 'for several widely different revolts against traditional philosophy' and that the three basic writers – Jaspers, Heidegger, and Sartre – are not in agreement on essentials. Such writers are linked by repudiation of systems and dissatisfaction with traditional philosophy – factors which bind them together in pre-occupations with failure, dread, and death (Kaufmann, p. 21). Kaufmann, however, reminds us that it was Rilke's *The Notes of Malte Laurids Brigge* (1910) which influenced Sartre's novel *Nausea* (see Kaufmann, pp. 113–20) and, above all, Kafka 'in whose major works and parables the absurdity of man's condition has found classical expression' (Kaufmann, p. 49).

But what must we understand by this label 'Existentialism'? Basically, for Sartre, it is the opposition between sincerity and Bad Faith. Bad Faith 'consists in pretending to ourselves and others that things could not be otherwise – that we are bound to our way of life, and that we could not escape it even if we wanted to' (Mary Warnock, *The Philosophy of Sartre*, p. 53). Most appeals, therefore, to duty or strong beliefs are seen by Sartre as instances of Bad Faith, since we are free to choose to do all these things, and we need not do them. This freedom, which brings anguish, springs from our recognition of Nothingness:

> To speak of the 'essence' of a thing is to speak of it as necessarily being as it is, and behaving as it does behave. Conscious beings have no essences. Instead of an essential core they have nothing. Beings-in-themselves have no possibilities; or rather, all their possibilities are realized at once at the moment of creation. From then on they behave as they were made to behave ... A conscious being, on the other hand, is aware of his own possibilities, of what he is not, or is not yet. So it comes about that he can pretend to be whatever he likes, and try to be whatever he likes.
>
> (Warnock, p. 62)

We aim, in Bad Faith, to evade the responsibilities of this condition by pretending to be *massif* – like Beings-in-themselves: the 'sincere' man faces Nothingness and experiences 'nausea' – the subject and title of Sartre's first novel.

La Nausée (1938) is now published by Penguin Books in a translation by Robert Baldick (1965). As the title of the first English edition suggested, it is the diary of Antoine Roquentin begun after his first experience of what Sartre calls 'nausea'. After a life of some activity, Roquentin has settled in the little town of Bouville, where for three years he has been working on a historical study of the Marquis de Rollebon. He lives entirely alone; an outsider. One day, as he stands on the sea-shore, he undergoes a disturbing sensation: as he holds a pebble he feels 'a sort of sweet disgust' which passes from the pebble into his hands – 'a sort of nausea in the hands' (*Nausea*, p. 22). Other experiences of the same kind assail him and he begins to fear objects though he is unable to decide whether it is he or they which have changed. Even in his work on the Marquis – where there is a great deal of 'evidence' – he finds himself baffled by a lack of firmness and consistency. He visits the local picture gallery where hang the portraits of all the town's notables who had lived without ever feeling that their lives were stale or unjustifiable, who, as Roquentin now recognizes, had lived in Bad Faith.

This loss of appearances – when a seat on which he is sitting could very well be a dead donkey (see *Nausea*, pp. 179–80) – is the source of nausea; existence has unveiled itself to Roquentin's vision:

> It had lost its harmless appearance as an abstract category: it was the very stuff of things, that root steeped in existence. Or rather the root, the park gates, the bench, the sparse grass on the lawn, all that had vanished; the diversity of things, their individuality, was only an appearance, a veneer. This veneer had melted, leaving soft, monstrous masses, in disorder – naked, with a frightening, obscene nakedness.
>
> (*Nausea*, p. 183)

Later, when Roquentin needs a word to express this revelation – the key to his Existence, his life, that word is Absurdity, an absolute not a relative thing:

> That root – there was nothing in relation to which it was not absurd. Oh, how can I put that in words? Absurd: irreducible, nothing – not even a profound, secret aberration of Nature – could explain that.
>
> (*Nausea*, p. 185)

The novel ends with Roquentin abandoning historical research in favour of a work of art, possibly a novel, which will make people ashamed of their uselessness.

Iris Murdoch, in her invaluable study of Sartre, points out that to understand Sartre is to understand something about the present time since he belongs to the three important movements of our time: the phenomenological, the existential, and the Marxist. *Nausea*, existing as it does on more than one level, examines an old and familiar metaphysical doubt, the relation of words to the things described:

> The circle does not exist; but neither does what is named by 'black' or 'table' or 'cold'. The relation of these words to their context of application is shifting and arbitrary. What does exist is brute and nameless, it escapes from the scheme of relations in which we imagine it to be rigidly enclosed, it escapes from language and science, it is more than and other than our description of it.
>
> (Murdoch, p. 13)

Roquentin discovers that unless our values are being constantly broken down and rebuilt, they may solidify, as language solidifies and kills our thoughts. For Sartre's argument involves not only perception, but also the language by which that perception is expressed, and, hopefully, communicated. In his essay, *What is Literature?* (1948, trans. Frechtman, 1950), Sartre prescribed what the contemporary writer *ought* to write and what ideals he *ought* to adopt:

> The function of a writer is to call a spade a spade. If words are sick, it is up to us to cure them. Instead of that, many writers live off this sickness. In many cases literature is a cancer of words . . . There is nothing more deplorable than the literary practice which, I believe, is called poetic prose and which consists of using words for the obscure harmonics which resound about them and which are made up of vague meanings which are in contradiction with the clear meanings. I know: the purpose of a number of writers was to destroy words as that of the surrealists was to destroy both the subject and the object; but it was the extreme point of the literature of consumption. But today, as I have shown, it is necessary to construct. If one starts deploring the inadequacy of language to reality . . . one makes oneself

an accomplice of the enemy, that is, of propaganda. Our first duty as a writer is thus to re-establish language in its dignity. After all, we think with words. We would be quite vain to believe that we are concealing ineffable beauties which the word is unworthy of expressing. And then I distrust the incommunicable; it is the source of all violence.

(What is Literature?, pp. 210–11.)

The hero of *Nausea* shows Sartre's view that language and the world are hopelessly divorced from one another; only by putting the writer into an 'extreme situation' can this separation be avoided (*What is Literature?*, p. 164).

Sartre himself was quick to suggest that Camus's novel *The Outsider* could be understood in terms of philosophy, Camus's *The Myth of Sisyphus*. The conflict which is the basis of Absurdity can be better demonstrated in the novel or drama than in intellectual discourse, but there remains the danger of not balancing art and philosophy, a danger Camus clearly perceived when he reviewed *Nausea* in *Alger républicain* in October 1938. If, Camus argues, a novel is never anything but philosophy put into images, the whole of that philosophy must pass into the images or it looks like a label stuck on, and both plot and character lose authenticity. In *Nausea* this balance has not been properly maintained. Moreover life is not necessarily tragic because it is wretched: Sartre's hero, he complains, insists on those aspects of man which he finds repugnant instead of basing his reasons for despair on certain signs of man's greatness. But, primarily, it is the lack of positive response which Camus seems to miss most (published in *Lyrical and Critical*, London, 1967, pp. 145–7).

The fact is that Sartre uses literature as a means to an end: the expression of his philosophical ideas. But in a novel we are dealing with a fictitious character, whose opinions may not be shared by his creator. Roquentin is no ordinary man: he has no friends, no family, no home, and no job – except the self-imposed task of writing a biography. If in the novel he comes to find his own existence nauseatingly inescapable, and that objects, too, exist in spite of themselves, without any special function, need we share that feeling? Sartre offers some hope – the record of a jazz tune. Roquentin believes that, if he could write a book like that tune, 'beautiful and hard as steel' (*Nausea*, p. 252), he might be saved. But the novel is, nevertheless, deeply pessimistic. Sartre's more recent work encourages us to read the book as a warning of what happens to a man who cuts himself off from society, but the early work of Sartre will not permit this. It seems fairly clear that Sartre is writing a highly personal account of his own experience (possibly based on taking mescalin) (see Colin Wilson, *The Outsider*, p. 116), and that Roquentin is intended to speak for us all when he insists that we must, if we are sincere, feel, when we look at the world, nausea, a sense of the absurd (or our own superfluity) and the anguish which follows these perceptions. Support for this can be found in Sartre's *L'Imaginaire* (1940) and *L'Être et le Néant* (1943) (see Philip Thody, *Jean-Paul Sartre*).

The image of nausea is a useful one. It is not intended to be regarded as either exaggerated or a metaphor; it is the same nausea that is produced by spoiled meat or fresh blood (*Being and Nothingness*, pp. 338–9); and our disgust turns to horror and dread when we realize what Sartre calls the 'viscosity' of things. This idea of 'viscosity' is difficult. Mary Warnock illustrates the viscous by referring us to treacle. Treacle is an ambiguous substance, half liquid, half solid: we can pick it up but it eludes us, having no boundaries. On the other hand, if we try to pour it away like liquid, it refuses to go. But viscosity, like nausea, may be a private obsession of Roquentin (or his creator), for it is a weakness of metaphysical description that it may or may not appeal, and if it does not we wonder why that particular idea or category was chosen (Warnock, p. 105). It is, however, clearly important to Sartre's description of the world and our place in it. If we are unable to pin down other people with labels (because they, too, have no essence and are free), we are more hopeful of material objects. But at certain moments these too prove recalcitrant, and when objects (by which we hope to realize our projects) lose their solidity, then the projects also fall into jeopardy. This sudden refusal of objects to remain as tools labelled for our use produces the related feeling of futility, of being superfluous. The perception that we ourselves are basically nothing and therefore free to choose, is intimately connected with this feeling of absurdity: what we value is wholly contingent – to pretend otherwise would be Bad Faith. We cannot pretend that there are any absolute moral laws to bind us, that any path of duty is mapped out for us, or that we can have a function or a mission: 'Human life is absurd, in that there can be no final justification for our projects. Everyone is *de trop*; everything is dispensable'(Warnock, p. 109).

If we agree to feel anguish and nausea at recognizing absurdity, how ought we to behave? to what extent are we free? *Nausea*, even more than Camus's novel *The Outsider*, must be regarded as final, and Sartre's problem was to find an equally convincing image for the idea of freedom which begins action after absurdity has been recognized. We can suggest that *Nausea* as a novel is a little too long and that some of its theorizing seems out of place, but the main objection is that the positive response, as in *The Outsider*, occurs too briefly and too late. It was in the theatre that Sartre presented heroes who seem to find some sort of solution, possibly because drama compelled him to write more as a technician than as a man with obsessions. His first two plays, *The Flies* (1943) and *Huis Clos* (1944) – originally called *Les Autres* – illustrate the early Sartre. The Second World War helped Sartre (as it helped Camus) to crystallize a more positive response just after absurdity had been defined. In *Baudelaire* (1946) and *Saint Genet* (1952) he is still writing about existential man; but, since in his plays, novels, and essays he had always given his sympathy to those excluded from or

ishing to overthrow bourgeois society, it comes as no surprise
at the answer appears to be Marxism and what Warnock tersely
escribes as 'the death of Sartrean existentialism' (p. 135). The
eo-Marxist Sartre of 1960 bears scant resemblance to the author
f *Nausea* and *The Flies* and need not concern us.

Philip Thody, in *Jean-Paul Sartre*, used *The Flies* to illustrate
Nausea, by pointing out that Orestes affirms man's freedom by
nowing, in Jupiter's words, 'their obscene and tasteless existence
hich is given them for no purpose'. *The Flies*, published in
tuart Gilbert's translation by Penguin (1962), was first performed
by permission of the German censor – in Paris in 1943. In *What is
Literature?* Sartre writes of the old theatre of character where
ituation had no other function than to put these more or less com-
lete figures into conflict and show them changing. Now, Sartre
elieves, we must return to the theatre of situation:

> No more character; the heroes are freedoms caught in a trap like all
> of us. What are the issues? Each character will be nothing but the
> choices of an issue and will equal no more than the chosen issues. It is
> to be hoped that all literature will become moral and problematic like
> this new theatre.
>
> *(What is Literature?*, p. 217)

The 'situation' of *The Flies* is the return to Argos of Orestes to
venge the murder of his father, Agamemnon, by killing his uncle
Aegisthus and his mother Clytemnestra. French audiences were
ccustomed to seeing contemporary events presented in a classical
ale, and, in 1943, the play obviously referred to the occupation of
France by Germany. But Sartre really wishes to show a man assum-
ng responsibility for an event even though it fills him with horror,
nd the traditional idea of fatality in the original helps to empha-
ize Sartre's insistence on liberty in his version.

Sartre shows Orestes returning, as an outsider, to his native
Argos, a city obsessively pre-occupied with the guilt of Agamemnon's murder. Because of this pre-occupation the Gods can

maintain their power over mankind and govern them throug
Aegisthus and Clytemnestra. Orestes, urged on to vengeance b
Electra, asks what is the right thing to do and is told by Jupite
to leave Argos undisturbed:

> So that is the Right Thing. To live at peace . . . always at perfe
> peace. I see. Always to say 'Excuse me', and 'Thank you'. That
> what's wanted, eh? . . . The Right Thing. *Their* Right Thing.
>
> (*The Flies*, p. 27)

To do right always seems to involve submission. But Orestes see
that he is free to choose, and he *chooses* to avenge his father. He
also learns that once man receives the idea of liberty the Gods a
powerless to intervene.

By contrast, Electra, who has tried earlier in the play to persuad
the people of Argos that men are born to be happy, not to live i
perpetual guilt, begins to weaken and, after the murder, whe
Jupiter offers to free her from the Furies if she will show remors
for the crime (and thus repeat the pattern of Aegisthus and Cly
temnestra) she repents and is received back into the world o
Jupiter's ordering. Orestes, however, accepts responsibility for h
own freely chosen action and, like the Pied Piper, leaves Argo
drawing the flies with him. He thus assumes not merely his ow
guilt, but also the guilt of Argos, enjoying a freedom that confer
only exile 'on the far side of despair'. Sartre here illustrates, in th
character of Orestes, the concept of being as play-acting. Becaus
consciousness is self-consciousness, one can never *be* anythin
without knowing, and the knowledge calls this quality into ques
tion. I am lazy means I know I am lazy; that is, I choose to be laz
(which is my own responsibility), not I do this because I am
through no fault of mine, lazy. According to Sartre there are thre
kinds of beings: objects have being 'in-itself'; people have bein
'for-itself' because they have consciousness whereas objects hav
not; and, finally, we all have being 'for-others' – which is to sa

hat we all exist in the eyes of other people and think of ourselves
on the evidence of what other people think of us. Sartre believes
hat if I am regarded admiringly I exist more than if I am looked at
contemptuously. Real love under such circumstances is impos-
ible, since each merely wants the other to give him more existence
by admiration! An agreement can be reached, but the presence of a
hird person would cause even so tentative an agreement to
ollapse. Hence the study of Orestes leads to *Huis Clos*. Orestes
earns that he must invent what he chooses to be as he goes along;
he is no longer commanded to vengeance by Apollo as in the
original (which makes it difficult to understand why Apollo's
Temple still shelters him in Act III of Sartre's play), he has to
choose whether or not to avenge his father's murder. But it must
be admitted that he does so in a manner reminiscent of a magical
gesture, and one which leads him to walk out rather than settle
down with his people to work out their future (see R. F. Jackson
in *Aspects of Drama and the Theatre*, pp. 33–70).

In *Huis Clos* (translated as *No Exit* or *In Camera*) there are,
ominously, three characters. They are dead, and in Hell – a Second
Empire drawing-room. Clearly Sartre is not examining the possibilities of life after death, but in taking material sufficient for three
boulevard dramas he shows us three characters seeking definition
in the eyes of one another. Each is unable to bear complete responsibility for his own acts and wishes to be recognized by the
others as having a character (i.e. an essence); but this makes each
dependant on the others, and when two of them come to some
agreement that agreement is immediately wrecked by the presence
of the third person. Their alibis and excuses are useless in a Hell
which is very literally other people. Man, then, is the *sum* of his
acts. The idea that he does something because he is that sort of
man is replaced with the idea that a man is or makes himself that
sort of man by doing such and such an act. He is Nothing, and in
action becomes conscious of that original Nothingness – the result

is anguish because he can no longer justify himself through faith or morals. He can, of course, fall back into blindness or Bad Faith, or he can 'assume his acts and his life, fully aware of the world's absurdity, and accept the crushing responsibility of giving the world a meaning that comes from himself alone' (Guicharnaud, *Modern French Theatre*, pp. 136–7).

5
Albert Camus[1]

The document most cited in discussions of Absurdity is a collection of essays called *The Myth of Sisyphus* by Albert Camus, who is still most widely known as the author of *The Outsider* and *The Myth*, philosopher of the Absurd and an existentialist. Camus denied, in an interview in 1951 that he was either a philosopher or an existentialist, and indeed said that *The Myth* was intended as a rebuke to so-called existentialists. Nevertheless, Guicharnaud, recalling his apprenticeship in existentialism, mentions Kafka, Sartre's *Nausea*, and Camus's *The Outsider*, as the works in which experience was rendered intelligible and given a name (*Sartre*, Twentieth Century Views, p. 15). If Absurdity has a long history, at least as far back as Ecclesiastes, the particular contemporary response is different possibly because Camus is not a philosopher and, if his thought seems to move in the same channels as that of Heidegger, Jaspers, or Sartre, it develops positively into something different. In 1938 Camus published *Noces* in which four basic themes emerge: the hopelessness of life, the need to 'refuse' the world without renouncing it, the purity of the heart, and happiness. *The Myth of Sisyphus* is an intellectual investigation of the attitude to life treated lyrically in *Noces*, but Camus still wishes to describe the feeling of Absurdity, not write a philosophy. The feeling of Absurdity, Camus says, could strike any man in the face at any street-corner. This sudden birth of feeling arrives generally in one of four ways (or several of them, of course):

[1] I am much indebted in this chapter to John Cruickshank, *Albert Camus and the Literature of Revolt.*

D

1. The mechanical nature of many people's lives may lead them to question the value and purpose of their existence; this is an intimation of absurdity.
2. An acute sense of time passing, or the recognition that time is a destructive force.
3. A sense of being left in an alien world. Camus suggests that a world which can be explained even with bad reasons is a familiar world. But in a world from which illusions and insight have been suddenly removed man feels himself a stranger. At its most intense this sense of alienation is carried to the point of nausea when familiar objects normally 'domesticated' by names – such as stone or tree – are also robbed of their familiarity.
4. A sense of isolation from other beings.

The Absurd, for Camus, is an absence of correspondence between the mind's need for unity and the chaos of the world the mind experiences, and the obvious response is either suicide or, in the opposite direction, a leap of faith.

Camus distinguishes two kinds of suicide, physical and philosophical (and under the latter heading he looks at previous philosophers who have recognized Absurdity – Jaspers, Husserl, Heidegger, for example – but have evaded it in one way or another), and rejects both. Man must accept the feeling of Absurdity, which then becomes a springboard for action, giving him a sense of freedom and passion. But, as Cruickshank points out, Camus has already given the word three different meanings during his demonstration: (i) the whole tragic paradox of the human condition and anguish (ii) which, as a source of lucidity, we are called upon to maintain as fully as we can to produce (iii) an attitude of revolt that somehow requires us to use 'absurd' (sense ii) against 'absurd' (sense i). This is both confusing and confused. It is as if Camus had taken the key to existence as not being given a key and made his own leap of faith! But Camus is not writing philosophy,

nd he *is* interested in consequences; the prime response is revolt.
ince in an Absurd world all things are equal, the ethic of revolt can
ecommend neither virtue nor crime, though it does not exclude
what we conventionally term virtuous.

Camus then offers us four models: Don Juan, the actor (whose
tage becomes a symbol of our universe enclosed with 'absurd
walls'), the conqueror and the artist, and he concludes with the
ssay which gives its name to the book: 'The Myth of Sisyphus' .It
s not clear why the man who, according to Homer, was the wisest
nd most prudent of mortals (but who, according to others, was a
rigand) was punished with so futile a labour in the Underworld.
Accounts vary as to the exact misdeeds of this cunning king of
Corinth, but the general impression emerges of a man who
corned the Gods, loved life, hated death, and was absurdly
unished. For Camus, the knowledge of this absurdity gives
Sisyphus victory: we must imagine Sisyphus happy.

Cruickshank is, I believe, correct when he says the essays leave
us dissatisfied. They make no suggestions as to what kind of moral
onduct revolt should give rise to, although, in fact, historical
vents (namely World War II) provided their author with positive
ecommendations. The philosophy of the Absurd also runs into
ontradictions as soon as it is expressed since any such expression
ssumes some coherence at the centre of the incoherence it sets out
o analyse. We shall increasingly have to recognize that a satis-
actory analysis of Absurdity would be total silence. Camus sees a
work of art as an absurd phenomenon, but one in which personal
awareness is brought out for others to see in the hope of making
hem aware also, and indicating the common fate. In this sense
here can and must be Absurd literature, and in Camus this can be
estricted (as Thomas Hanna restricts it in his study *The Thought
nd Art of Albert Camus*) to *The Outsider* and the two plays
Caligula and *Cross Purpose*.

L'Étranger was completed in 1939, a year before Camus finished

The Myth, and both were published within months of one another in 1942. It is available in England translated by Stuart Gilbert under the title *The Outsider*, published by Penguin, with the original introduction by Cyril Connolly of 1946. Connolly, too, groups it with *The Myth* and the two plays as literature of the Absurd, but reminds us that Camus is an Algerian, and that a characteristically Mediterranean love of life and youth is present to balance absurdity and death. He aptly quotes Camus as writing that if there is a sin of life 'it is not perhaps so much to despair of life, as to hope for another life and to lose sight of the implacable grandeur of this one.' Mr Connolly also points out that the basic absurdity of the novel is the application of Christian morality and a European code of justice to a non-European people – which is to say that Absurdity here is social, not metaphysical, in its origins.

The story of *The Outsider* is simple. Meursault's mother is dead, and although there has been, for some time, no meaningful relationship between them, he attends her wake and funeral. He returns to Algiers, where he goes swimming, meets a girl and, after taking her to see a comic film, begins a love affair with her. Rather passively, he accepts the confidences and friendship of a man living in the same apartment block, and this involvement culminates in the shooting of an Arab on the beach.

At his trial, Meursault's conduct is described by the Prosecutor as that of an unfeeling, hardened criminal, who, moreover, had associated with undesirable people. He is found guilty and sentenced to decapitation. His explanation of the shooting – that it was because of the sun (to which he is particularly sensitive) – only produces a titter in the courtroom. While he waits for execution he is visited, against his wishes, by the prison chaplain, whose attitude finally stirs Meursault out of his total indifference. He recognizes the worthlessness of the chaplain's so-called certainties and the social and religious ideas that he stands for:

What difference could they make to me, the death of others, or a mother's love, or his God; or the way one decides to live, the fate one thinks one chooses, since one and the same fate was bound to 'choose' not only me but thousands of millions of privileged people who, like him, called themselves my brothers. Surely, surely he must see that? Every man alive was privileged; there was only one class of men, the privileged class. All alike would be condemned to die one day; his turn, too, would come like the others. And what difference could it make if, after being charged with murder, he were executed because he didn't weep at his mother's funeral, since it all came to the same thing in the end . . .

(*The Outsider*, pp. 118–19)

A close connection between *The Outsider* and *The Myth* was persuasively established by Sartre in his 'explication' of the novel which appeared in February 1943, and was published by Gallimard in *Situations I* (1947). This remarkable essay begins by asking how we can understand a character like Meursault and Sartre's reply is that Camus has provided, in *The Myth* which was published several months later, a precise commentary on the novel. This hero is neither good nor wicked, moral nor immoral, he is what Camus calls 'absurd'. Sartre then provides an explanation of the Absurd, reminding us that the novel does not explain; it merely *describes* the condition and its consequences. Passing to its sources and the current description that it was a novel of Kafka written by Hemingway, he suggests that no one could be further from Kafka than Camus. For Kafka the universe is full of signs we cannot understand, whereas for Camus the human predicament stems from the absence of any such signs. But Hemingway is an obvious influence. Sartre concludes that Camus chose the style because it was the most appropriate; it confers an equality on everything, just as in an absurd world everything is of equal value. So the flatness of the style refuses to emphasize anything more or less than anything else; but Sartre also, perceptively, doubts whether or not such a style will be useful to Camus in subsequent novels.

Cruickshank agrees with this verdict. The first person narrative— usually so individual and subjective – is here flat and objective (because Meursault is the opposite of the traditional first-person nineteenth-century narrator); where a treatise would have to explain, the novel can merely record experiences which rely on failure to explain for their meaning:

> The first-person narrative gives an impression of authentic direct- ness. The severely restricted vocabulary prevents analytical direct- ness. And by bringing authentic directness and lack of analytical power together in the same character Camus conveys a strong im- pression of the void felt by someone who experiences the absurd.
>
> (Cruickshank, p. 154)

On the one occasion rhetorical prose is used (the murder scene) the rhetoric serves to convey mistrust and demonstrate how it obscures the real nature of the experience. Any further novels using this technique would simply repeat the first.

Thomas Hanna, however, offers a different emphasis. He points out that, strictly speaking, Meursault shows the indifference of an absurd hero without the hero's consciousness of absurdity, and the element of revolt appears very late in the book. It is indifference which makes him a stranger. In the first part, neither we nor, for that matter, the other characters feel that he is outside. The murder forces an absolute judgement to be made on him and his drifting world comes into collision with the world of absolute values. It is, therefore, moral legalism which has insisted upon fixed values in a sphere which has none – human life – which destroys Meursault. *The Outsider* shows the divorce between the attempts to live honestly in accordance with the indeterminate nature of human existence and an attempt to impose general moral values on that indeterminate nature. It is only at the end that the visit of the chap- lain stimulates the response of revolt, freedom, and passion.

After *The Outsider* Camus wrote two plays. Considering that Absurdity depends upon conflict and confrontation and that serious French drama is characterized by an attempt to treat contemporary problems and prescribe remedies, this is not surprising. *Caligula* and *Cross Purpose* (both plays translated by Stuart Gilbert) are published together by Penguin, with an excellent introduction by John Cruickshank. *Caligula,* originally written in 1938 and reworked in 1945 and 1958, is a play based on material borrowed from the historian Suetonius. Camus, however, *interprets* the sudden reversal of character which turned a good Emperor into a monster after the death of the Emperor's sister, Drusilla, as a revelation of the Absurd.

The play opens after the death of Drusilla (with whom the Emperor has had an incestuous relationship); the Emperor has disappeared and the patricians are perturbed by his absence. When he returns, tired and untidy, he assures them that he is not mad, rather he has never felt so lucid in his life, for he has discovered a simple truth:

'Men die; and they are not happy.'

The inescapable nature of death renders all things equally unimportant, and the Emperor intends, since his power to do so is absolute, to undeceive a world he now sees as full of 'lies and self-deception'. His actions henceforth are intended to reveal to everyone the nature of Absurdity; and from the point of view of his motives, Caligula is neither evil nor tyrannical, but rather an idealist following his new idea or truth to its logical conclusion. Thus his new reign is one of caprice and whim: executions, famine, extortion, and immorality – in which he uses the wives of patricians as prostitutes, exposes the patricians to ridiculous art contests (while, off-stage, people are being slaughtered): everything is equal. Against Meursault there was an array of lawyers; against Caligula one character emerges, Cherea. Cherea fights Caligula not because he is afraid to lose his life, but because Caligula's actions deny that life has any meaning; when the two argue in Act III, Cherea repeats this, that he cannot live in a world where the absurd can 'transfix their lives, like a dagger in the heart', and when Caligula accuses him of shrinking from the truth of Absurdity he simply replies:

> Because what I want is to live, and be happy. Neither, to my mind, is possible if one pushes the absurd to its logical conclusions. As you see, I'm quite an ordinary sort of man. True, there are moments when, to feel free of them, I desire the death of those I love, or hanker after women from whom the ties of family or friendship debar me. Were logic everything, I'd kill or fornicate on such occasions. But I consider these passing fancies of no great importance. If everyone set to gratifying them, the world would be impossible to live in, and happiness, too, would go by the board. And these, I repeat, are the things that count, for me.

Cherea believes that some actions are 'more praiseworthy than others'; but Caligula believes that all actions are of equal importance and acts accordingly, and he has, therefore, to be destroyed.

Cross Purpose (Le Malentendu) appeared in 1944, but its source is in *The Outsider*. Meursault in prison finds a yellow bit of newspaper under his mattress with the story of a crime committed unknowingly by a woman and her daughter against a stranger who turned out to be her son. Camus changes the details slightly in the play, but would probably agree with Meursault's comment: 'Anyhow, to my mind, the man was asking for trouble; one shouldn't play fool tricks of that sort' (*The Outsider*, p. 82). Like Orestes, the hero Jan returns unrecognized to his mother and sister who keep an inn. In spite of the doubts of his wife, Maria, he insists on staying the night alone there, incognito, so that he can get to know them better. Martha and her mother, however, wish to escape from Europe and have gathered money by murdering visitors to the inn, and, although they feel curiously attracted to Jan, they try not to get to know him. Just as he is prepared to abandon the experiment, he drinks the poisoned tea and the mother realizes that it is too late. When they discover the truth, the mother recognizes that the world they live in makes no sense at all, and that only by killing herself can she prove the existence of one certainty: mother love. Martha, however, is stirred to revolt. It seems to her unfair that she should be robbed of dream, brother, and mother:

> I hate this narrow world in which we are reduced to gazing up at God. But I have not been given my rights and I am smarting from the injustice done me; I will not bend my knee. I have been cheated of my place on earth, cast away by my mother, left alone with my crimes, and I shall leave this world without being reconciled.

She can honestly say to Maria that words like 'love', 'joy' and 'grief' are meaningless, and as she leaves to kill herself, Maria is left with only God to appeal to: without His help the world is a 'desert'. But her cries attract only the old manservant, who replies to her appeal for help in a clear, firm tone: No.

As Cruickshank points out in his introduction, in *Caligula* Camus describes an individual's possibly mistaken response to the discovery of the Absurd, but in *Cross Purpose* it is injustice and misunderstanding built into the world as we know it which renders individuals helpless and unhappy. *Cross Purpose* is, therefore, the more pessimistic play. It emphasizes that human beings cannot communicate, that death is inevitable, that solitude and exile haunt everyone, that there is probably no solution at all (Introduction, Penguin edition, p. 23). Both plays belong to the most negative period of Camus's thought. Thus, although the form of *Cross Purpose* – its simplicity and directness, the observance of the classical unities so much admired in French theatre, the absence of side-issues and the careful planning of events – would seem to deny the message of the play, that message remains nevertheless that human beings are caught up in the absurdity of existence, and doomed to separation and exile, with just a hint of the revolt that develops in Camus's later plays.

In the novel that followed *The Outsider*, *The Plague* (written in

1944–7), the focus, despite the title, has been shifted to resistance. It is true that the plague provides the novel with a closed universe and a sense of absurdity and death, but Camus is moving towards his statement of the counter-idea of revolt which emerges in *The Rebel* (1951); revolt has not produced anything which negates the Absurd, but man does learn that he can, without help from God, create his own values and pass beyond the anguish which is the terminus of existential revolt. Hanna, therefore, is correct in describing *The Myth* as an absurdist experiment from which Camus developed because of his feeling for men who suffer in the absurd world. That all men die is a problem we can do very little about, but that all men are oppressed is a condition we can ameliorate. Thus the Algerian love of life qualifies the pessimism: the Absurd is a beginning not an end (see Hanna, p. 103).

Jean-Paul Sartre has insisted that he and Camus use the word 'Absurd' differently, but the difference in usage appears to be slight, and in the history of French theatre Sartre and Camus belong together, because they both subscribe to the belief that acts alone are important. Both writers believe that violence is a characteristic of our age, hence in the plays of both isolation and violence are the two salient features. Whereas Sartre's plays tend to start in a world of common sense and lead the spectator to an existentialist conclusion, Camus tends to begin early, as in *Caligula*, with that discovery: but both, in their early work, illustrate existential doctrines *consistently*, and this gives them an importance greater than other dramatists in whom traces of existentialism can be detected.

6
Revolt

There is nothing new in considering the world purposeless and chaotic, and it is not even certain that the feeling of Absurdity in the twentieth century is, in fact, exceptionally widespread. It is certain, however, that as a feeling it is at its best transitory – it begins something. Valery's comment, that at least Sisyphus got well-developed muscles out of his absurd labours, is not quite the hollow joke it might at first seem. Even as we define the Absurd condition, we undermine its validity, and, even as we speak of the anguish which is our common fate, Sisyphus begins to assume Promethean qualities indicative of our response. Absurdity and Revolt are very closely linked in the *ideal* pattern. Thus David Grossvogel, in *Four Playwrights and a Postscript* (1962), is able to discuss Brecht, Ionesco, Beckett, and Genet together, not by making Brecht an Absurdist, but by showing that all four are angry as much with what goes on in the theatre as with what is wrong in the world that theatre is supposed to reflect. In his book *The Theatre of Revolt* (1965) Robert Brustein claims that the usual critical treatment – under the headings of Realism, Naturalism, Symbolism – disguises an essential unity in writers such as Ibsen, Strindberg, Brecht, Genet, and George Bernard Shaw. All in their own ways revolt at the absurdity of the human condition. Like most American critics, Brustein sees literature in patterns, and finds three types of revolt, the third of which he calls 'existential', and which uses the ironic mode:

> In the ironic mode, the word 'hero' has lost its meaning entirely – the central figure is 'inferior in power and intelligence to ourselves so that we have a sense of looking down on a scene of bondage, frustration

or absurdity'. This is the scene of the antihero – usually a tramp, a proletarian, a criminal, an old man, a prisoner, confined in body and spirit, and deteriorating in his confinement . . . For in existential drama, nature, society, man no longer exist. In this final phase of the modern drama – in these nightmares, chimeras, hallucinations, and feverish fables – revolt finds its most pessimistic, contracted, and exhausted form.

(Brustein, pp. 31–2)

We are seeking this final phase, when the form is Absurd. Esslin, noticeably, does not use the plays of Sartre or Camus in his discussion of the Theatre of the Absurd. He argues that such a theatre should, properly, try to achieve a unity between its basic assumptions and the form in which they are expressed, so the theatre of Sartre and Camus is to him a 'less adequate expression of the philosophy . . . than the Theatre of the Absurd' (Esslin, p. 24). He points out that Camus uses 'the elegantly rationalistic and discursive style of an eighteenth-century morality, in well-constructed and polished plays', while Sartre presents his ideas in plays 'based on brilliantly drawn characters who remain wholly consistent and thus reflect the old convention that each human being has . . . an immortal soul.' Both, by implication, proclaim tacitly that logic can offer solutions, that language, analysed, will lead to basic concepts. Absurd Theatre does not argue, it presents (Esslin, pp. 24–5). But we could legitimately object that where Absurdity is concerned all art is a compromise with silence, and that the extent of the compromise is, perhaps, not very important; or that in *Nausea* and *The Outsider* Sartre and Camus *have* matched form and content. That they did not do so in drama involves us in a look at recent French drama.

Eric Bentley, in *The Playwright as Thinker*, divides modern drama into realism and anti-realism, and suggests that, according to our point of view, modern drama begins in 1730, 1830, or 1880, with a fourth important start in the years 1900–25, when the theatre began to reflect the important changes consequent upon the invention of the cinema and electric light. In 1887 Antoine founded his Théâtre Libre (championing realism and naturalism) and in 1891 Paul Fort's Théâtre d'Art championed the so-called 'Poetic' theatre; but the greatest challenge to realism in France came not from this 'Poetic' theatre, but from the Wagnerians, the supporters of dancing, music, and design. From 1890 onwards it is directors and theorists who are the most important agents in the theatre; and Alfred Jarry.

Gabriel Brunet has written of Jarry that his life seemed to have been directed by a philosophical concept:

> He offered himself as a victim to the derision and to the absurdity of the world. His life is a sort of humorous and ironic epic which is carried to the point of the voluntary, farcical and thorough destruction of the self. Jarry's teaching could be summarized thus: every man is capable of showing his contempt for the cruelty and stupidity of the universe by making his own life a poem of incoherence and absurdity.
>
> (Quoted in the introduction to *Ubu Roi*, *New Directions* (1961))

Just as *The Bald Prima Donna* (1950) ushered in an era that we call Absurd Drama, so theatre everywhere has never been the same since the first word of *Ubu Roi* was spoken by Fermin Gémier at the Théâtre Nouveau on 10 December 1896. *Ubu Roi* is a typical fairy-tale turned sour. At the beginning of the play, Ubu, a grotesquely fat, dirty, cruel person is being urged by his wife to kill Wenceslas, the king of Poland, and usurp the throne. Ubu had formerly been the king of Aragon, but is now captain of Wenceslas's dragoons. The next day Ubu butchers the king and all the royal family (except the heir Bougrelas and his mother who escape). He rules by killing anyone who has money so that he can have it all himself; thus we see a long procession of noblemen, judges and financiers fall into his 'disembraining' machine. When he has amassed all the money in the realm, he sets off to fight the czar of Russia who has sworn to avenge the death of his cousin Wenceslas. Ubu is defeated and sails, with his wife, for France. Jarry followed this with *Ubu Cocu* (written about 1897 or 1898) where Ubu, a private man, demonstrates that his character is unchanged. He is still evil personified, crushing anyone in his path and doing just what he pleases. A third play, *Ubu Enchaîné* – as formless and haphazard as ever – shows Ubu deciding to be a slave and reversing the usual values of slavery and liberty. If *Ubu Roi* was a parody of *Macbeth*, this last, as its title suggests, was a parody of Aeschylus's *Prometheus Bound*.

The plots do not, obviously, convey the attack the plays made against the conventions of current drama and every value bourgeois society maintains. *Ubu Roi* divided Paris into Ubuists and anti-Ubuists – with the latter in a large majority. The only critic who wrote a favourable review of the play lost his job next day! Jarry's rebellion was against everything: physical and metaphysical – to the point of inventing a new 'reality' and thus creating the science of 'Pataphysics – the science of imaginary solutions. Fortunately, as Wellwarth remarks, Jarry was neither a practical nor an active person, and his revolt was only seminal and instinctive. It heralds the work of the 1950s but, as Pronko perceptively objects, the anarchy in *Ubu Roi* is man-made and, presumably, can be corrected by man. *Ubu Roi* is a play that 'suggests little of an ontological nature' and exhibits no feeling that language is meaningless (Pronko, *Avant-Garde*, pp. 6–7).

The movement of irrational theatre became more organized under Apollinaire, who was much influenced by Jarry and who began writing a 'play' called *Les Mamelles de Tirésias* in 1903 – although it was not completed until 1917. In that year Diaghilev had produced *Parade* (scenario by Cocteau, music by Satie, costumes and décor by Picasso, and choreography by Massine), which affronted the Parisian audiences (for reasons not altogether artistic); and in June, at the Théâtre Maubel, the curtain rose on a play (opera or ballet) called *Les Mamelles de Tirésias*. In the preface Apollinaire protests against the stage illusion, calling his play *un drama surréaliste* (and thus coining the word) and the Prologue lays down a new theatrical procedure:

> On tente ici d'infuser un esprit nouveau au théâtre
> Une joie une volupté une vertu
> Pour remplacer ce pessimisme vieux de plus d'un siècle
> Ce qui est bien ancien pour une chose si ennuyeuse
> La pièce a été faite pour une scène ancienne
> Car on ne nous aurait pas construit de théâtre nouveau
> Un théâtre rond à deux scènes
> Une au centre l'autre formant comme un anneau
> Autour des spectateurs et qui permettra
> Le grand déploiement de notre art moderne
> Mariant souvent sans lien apparent comme dans la vie
> Les sons les gestes les couleurs les cris les bruits
> La musique la danse l'acrobatie la poésie la peinture
> Les choeurs les actions et les décors multiples. . . .

(Here we try to bring into the theatre a new spirit, a joy, a voluptuousness, a virtue to replace that pessimism which is more than a century old, which for a thing so wearying is quite old. The play was made for an old-fashioned stage because they would not let us build a new theatre, a theatre in the round with two stages, one in the centre the other like a ring round the spectators which would allow us to make a big deployment of our modern art marrying – often without apparent links as in life – sounds, gestures, colours, cries, noises, music, dancing, acrobatics, poetry, painting, choruses, actions, and multiple décors . . .)

And what did the 'New Spirit' present to its audience on that one and only performance of Apollinaire's work? The curtain rose to reveal a market place in Zanzibar; in the background an actor dressed to represent the people of Zanzibar, surrounded by musical instruments which were to accompany the declaiming actors; in the foreground Theresa – dressed in the symbols of a housewife

(pots, pans, brooms) having a furious quarrel with her husband
Theresa is bored with life as a woman, tired of being docile and
obedient and bearing children. She wants to become a soldier
Member of Parliament, or Cabinet Minister, but above all to have
no more children. At this moment a beard appears on her face,
her vast bosom opens to reveal balloons which she throws at the
audience as she declares that she is now a man, called Tiresias. She
forces her husband to change clothes with her and resists his arguments on the importance of giving birth to children. He ends by
deciding to do it himself since she will not. The choir intervenes
musically and the second scene opens with the husband in the
market place nursing his children. In eight days he has given birth
to 40,051 and the country is now threatened with famine. A sterile
policeman comes to arrest him and end the dangerous situation,
and their argument is interrupted by the arrival of a fortune-teller
who praises fecundity, and in the ensuing struggle is revealed as
Theresa who has returned home repentant. The policeman, immediately converted, promises that he, too, will have numerous
children and the curtain falls.

Some critics frankly enjoyed themselves, but others were moved
to righteous anger by the experiment; possibly this induced
Apollinaire to write a rather solemn preface claiming that his play
was propaganda for an increased birth rate on which the pros-
perity of a nation depended! A joke, perhaps. In form surrealist,
this unique experiment may have liberated through anarchy (as
Cocteau claimed), but it also subscribed to a noble and moral intention – producing an enjoyable ambiguity. Apollinaire died in
the autumn of 1918. The works of Dada and Surrealism are few
(one critic lists thirteen plays, chiefly short works by men mainly
working in poetry or the novel), and after the first shock the movement subsided until 1950. Like the German Expressionists, these
writers tried to grapple with difficult problems, but, as Eric Bentley succinctly puts it, Experimental theatre 'came to suggest the

merely brilliant, the technically clever, the assiduously heterodox, the forever incomplete' (*The Playwright as Thinker*, pp. 194–5). Ionesco, in an interview for the B.B.C. Third Programme in 1960, cited *Les Mamelles* as one of the works that most impressed him – but it is the insistence on spectacle, the use of the theatre *differently*, which bring us to the most important influence, Artaud.

Artaud, as L. R. Chambers says, is no myth, although current history is making him into one. Born in 1896, he died of cancer in Paris in 1948 (*see Aspects of Drama and Theatre*, pp. 115–42). A lively figure in the theatre between the two world wars, declared insane in 1938 (under mysterious circumstances), he spent the war years in various asylums. His main contribution is a series of manifestos concerning the theatre, published in 1938 under the title *The Theatre and its Double* by Gallimard (published, New York, 1958, in a translation by Mary C. Richards). Chambers points out that Artaud's theatre forces us to break through the thin veneer of contingency which allows us to feel secure, and that there are passages that parallel the more famous examples in Sartre's *Nausea*, also published in 1938.

The manifesto opens with a description of the effects of plague on society and compares the true theatre and its effect with the plague: which 'disturbs the senses' repose, frees the repressed unconscious, incites a kind of revolt (which moreover can have its full effect only if it remains virtual), and imposes on the assembled collectivity an attitude that is both difficult and heroic (Artaud, p. 28). The *true* theatre to do this is, according to Artaud, not Occidental but Oriental – a view arising from the impression he retained of Balinese dancers seen at the Colonial Exhibition in 1932. Words, therefore, are not important: mime, gesture and scenery are. It is a theatre 'which eliminates the author in favour of what we would call, in our Occidental theatrical jargon, the director; but a director who has become a kind of manager of magic, a master of sacred ceremonies' (Artaud, p. 60). There must

E

be no more masterpieces since what was good for the past is no good for the present, which demands a *theatre of cruelty*:

> With this mania we all have for depreciating everything, as soon as I have said 'cruelty', everybody will at once take it to mean 'blood'. But '*theater* of cruelty' means a theater difficult and cruel for myself first of all. And, on the level of performance, it is not the cruelty we can exercise upon each other by hacking at each other's bodies, carving up our personal anatomies . . . but the much more terrible and necessary cruelty which things can exercise against us. We are not free. And the sky can still fall on our heads. And the theatre has been created to teach us that first of all.
>
> (Artaud, p. 79)

The number of times Artaud feels it necessary to repudiate sadism suggests that he is aware of the difficulty. The basic idea of 'cruelty' remains puzzling not so much in defining the kind of play it produces, as in limiting the implications of the word itself correctly. The spectator must be compelled to recognize the cruel universe (as Artaud saw it) and the cruelty dormant in himself. The scenes were calculated to purge the spectator rather than move him to imitate, but he should be shocked into recognizing that certainties are deceptions. Thus, as in tragedy (but lacking the nobility of the tragic pattern), violence, blood, torture, and plague are useful, but more importantly, as adjuncts to what Charles Marowitz has called the cruellest of all practices: 'the exposure of mind, heart, and nerve-ends to the gruelling truths behind a social reality that deals in psychological crises when it wants to be *honest*, and political evils when it wants to be *responsible*, but rarely if ever confronts the existential horror behind all social and psychological facades' ('British Theatre', *Tulane Drama Review*, p. 172).

This effect Artaud hoped to create by the use of spectacle:
Every spectacle will contain a physical and objective element, perceptible to all. Cries, groans, apparitions, surprises, theatricalities of all kinds, magic beauty of costumes taken from certain ritual models;

resplendent lighting, incantational beauty of voices, the charms of harmony, rare notes of music, colors of objects, physical rhythms of movements whose crescendo and decrescendo will accord exactly with the pulsation of movements familiar to everyone, concrete appearances of new and surprising objects, masks, effigies yards high, sudden changes of light, the physical action of light which arouses sensations of heat and cold ...

(Artaud, p. 93)

This is Apollinaire's programme intensified; and for Artaud words will occupy the place and importance they have in dreams. Moreover, the distinction between stage and auditorium will be completely abolished.

We can now see much of Artaud's intention fulfilled in our contemporary theatre, as in the Aldwych production of the *Marat-Sade*, or the recent production at the National Theatre of Seneca's *Oedipus*, but the only opportunity for Artaud to put his theories in practice came between 1927–9, when he and Roger Vitrac ran their own theatre, significantly named the Théâtre Alfred Jarry. His influence, particularly his insistence on dream techniques, has been considerable in the Theatre of the Absurd, but Absurd dramatists (with the possible exception of the later Beckett) have ignored his ideas about eliminating the author and his text. Indeed, Absurd Theatre has been prominently a theatre of playwrights rather than producers.

7
The School of Paris

What separates the drama of the Absurd from the drama of the twenties is an absence of the picturesque shock and scandal which the early writers cultivated, the presence of a more serious purpose than ever emerged from the Surrealists, and a wider audience. This more serious purpose (and wider audience) stems from the existential basis laid down by Camus and Sartre. Now Man is seen more clearly as having, if he is honest, no purpose. Although he can and does get trapped in fixed ideas about himself and the world which turn him into a thing rather than a being, he finds the over-abundance of things, which limits freedom, nauseating and recognizes that just as habit conceals his attitudes, so language, too, has become a dead thing, limiting communication and emphasizing his solitude. He can no longer think that he has a nature proper to himself; he is simply the sum of his actions, each of which is a deliberate choice in a given situation.

Such writers, inevitably, are a heterogeneous group, sharing only a refusal to codify, which matches as far as possible their generally held beliefs. Thus Ionesco can truthfully say that there is no *avant-garde* theatre. To use the name 'The School of Paris', therefore, is misleading, for it suggests community and organization, while to call them the generation of the fifties would be too loose. Pronko (as the title of his book shows) prefers '*avant-garde*' rather than either of these labels, or Absurd (which would exclude a writer like Schehadé), but to my mind '*avant-garde*' shares disadvantages with the other terms (see Pronko, *Avant-Garde*, pp. 19–20), and 'The School of Paris' is fairly appropriate and, moreover, recalls that group of Cubists in the twenties who were

also expatriates: Picasso, Gris, Picabia, Severini, Marinetti and, of
course, Apollinaire.

IONESCO

In 1938 (that significant year) Eugène Ionesco received a govern-
ment grant to work in Paris on a thesis entitled 'Themes of Sin and
Death in French Literature since Baudelaire'. When the war
ended he was almost thirty-three and there was no sign that he was
going to become a dramatist. The story of how he began to learn
English by the Assimil method and rediscovered truths that he had
never thought about before (such as that the ceiling was up and the
floor was down), and that as the lesson progressed two characters
were introduced, Mr and Mrs Smith, whose conversation formed
itself into a play, is fully told by Esslin as is the account of how a
slip of the tongue by the actor playing the fire chief during
rehearsals gave the play the title by which we now know it:
La Cantatrice Chauve, translated as *The Bald Prima Donna* in
England, and *The Bald Soprano* in the United States (see Esslin,
pp. 134 ff.). It was not, however, until four years later, with
Amedée (1954), that Ionesco gained a large audience. More than
any other dramatist of this group, Ionesco has written notes and
explanation, and can be considered as the unofficial spokesman of
the 'movement'. The famous controversy with Kenneth Tynan in
1958 (fully discussed in Esslin, Chapter 3), shows the seriousness
of Ionesco's commitment to drama. R. N. Coe has called him 'the
most characteristic protagonist' of the Absurd (R. N. Coe,
'Eugène Ionesco: "The Meaning of UnMeaning",' *Aspects of
Drama and the Theatre*), and points out that in spite of a slender
and uneven output he has been remarkably popular. As his work
progresses the nightmarish quality asserts very strongly the basic
theme of death: 'I have no other images of the world, aside from
those which express evanescence and hardness, vanity and anger,

nothingness or hideous and useless hate. Existence has continued to appear to me in this way. Everything has only confirmed what I have seen, what I have understood in my childhood: vain and sordid furors, cries suddenly stifled by silence, shadows swallowed up forever in night' (quoted Pronko, *Avant-Garde*, p. 62). Ionesco, then, is concerned with two things: the human condition and how to present it in the theatre.

He has been much criticized, notably by Tynan, because he has no message; one of his favourite quotations is Nabokov's reply to this charge: No, I am a writer, I am *not a postman*. Not only is there an absence of social preaching, but his basic ideas resist proper expression in words. Indeed, R. N. Coe insists that we can best begin to understand them by a comparison with Zen Buddhism, where Nirvana is defined in terms of what is not and it is understood that if life has a meaning, that meaning must be irrational and incapable of expression. The Western mind, seduced by its reliance on rationalism, must reject any concept that cannot be proved rationally, but, Coe argues, rationalism is at the moment at something of a dead end. It can demolish (i.e. demonstrate as meaningless), but this only leaves Nothing, and with this Nothing is the Absurd.

Ionesco himself has tended to suggest that the opposite of Absurd is Meaningful, and that Absurdity is there to draw attention to a lack of meaning, but in fact the negative quality of his early plays merely reflects the general tendency of Western thought for the last two centuries, to deny the validity of such basic ideas as Aristotle's law on non-contradiction, the principle of causality and the factor of continuity. It is science, not the mystics, which has described the world as it is. Gide had to look for *l'acte gratuit*, but for Ionesco, in our time, all acts are gratuitous (and therefore nothing is more surprising than anything else); man is free and must bear responsibility. This Ionesco's hero, Berenger, tries to do, although on the whole Ionesco is not much bothered with the idea of 'responsibility' – to whom and for what in an Absurd universe? Thus, Coe points out, at the same time that the Existentialists have concluded that self is Nothingness which can only 'become' through acts and words, scientists have suggested that all acts are meaningless, and philologists (with the logical positivists) have shown that language, too, is arbitrary and meaningless as a means to the knowledge of reality (Coe, p. 24). These discoveries, however, have not generated despair; they have produced positive results and undermined the comfortable doctrine: *Ex nihilo nihil fit.*

We must not, however, burden Ionesco with the whole of Existential philosophy from Kierkegaard on (see Bentley, *The Life of the Drama*, p. 341). Ionesco is a dramatist who is concerned both with life and with illusion in the theatre. It was corruptness in the theatre, as he saw it, which finally pushed him to enter it in order that he might alter it:

To push the theatre beyond that intermediate zone which is neither theatre nor literature, is to restore it to its proper frame, to its natural limits. It was necessary not to hide the strings, but to make them even more visible, deliberately evident, to go all the way in the grotesque, in caricature, beyond the pale irony of witty drawing-room comedies. Not drawing-room comedies, but farce, an extreme burlesque exaggeration. Humor, yes, but with the methods of burlesque. A hard comedy, without finesse, excessive. No dramatic comedies either. But a return to the intolerable. Push everything to a state of paroxysm, there where the sources of tragedy lie. Create a theatre of violence: violently comic, violently dramatic.

Avoid psychology, or rather give it a metaphysical dimension. Theatre is an extreme exaggeration of feelings, an exaggeration which disjoints the real. It is also the dislocation and disarticulation of language.

('Discovering the Theatre', *The Theatre in the Twentieth Century*, ed. Corrigan, pp. 77–93. The quotation is on p. 85.)

In *Victims of Duty* Nicholas D'Eu outlines an ideal theatre:

> The theatre of my dreams would be irrationalist . . . The contemporary theatre is, indeed, still a prisoner of outmoded forms, it's never got beyond the psychology of a Paul Bourget . . . the contemporary theatre doesn't reflect the cultural tone of our period, it's not in harmony with the general drift of the other manifestations of the modern spirit . . . I should introduce contradiction where there is no contradiction, and no contradiction where there is what common sense usually calls contradiction. . . . We'll get rid of the principle of identity and unity of character and let movement and dynamic psychology take its place . . . We are not ourselves . . . Personality doesn't exist. Within us there are only forces that are either contradictory or not contradictory . . . as for plot and motivation, let's not mention them. We ought to ignore them completely, at least in their old form, which was too clumsy, too obvious . . . too . . . phoney, like anything that's too obvious. . . . No more drama, no more tragedy: the tragedy's turning comic, the comic is tragic, and life's getting more cheerful. . . .
>
> (*Plays*, Vol. 2, trans. Donald Watson,
> London, 1958, pp. 307–9)

Such a theatre, illustrated by *The Bald Prima Donna*, is, however, rejected by the Detective, who insists on remaining 'Aristotelically logical, true to myself, faithful to my duty and full of respect for my bosses':

> I don't believe in the absurd, everything hangs together, everything can be comprehended in time . . . thanks to the achievements of human thought and science.
>
> (*Plays*, vol. 2, p. 309)

The Bald Prima Donna is subtitled 'An Anti-Play'. The stage directions begin:

> A typical middle-class English interior. Comfortable armchairs. Typical English evening at home. Typical English MR SMITH, in his favorite armchair, wearing English slippers, smoking an English pipe, reading an English newspaper, beside an English fire. He is

wearing English spectacles, has a small grey English moustache. Next to him in *her* favorite armchair, typically English MRS SMITH is darning English socks. A long English silence. An English clock chimes three English chimes.

The rather odd conversation between these two characters leads Mr Smith to decide they should go to bed when Mary, who claims to be the maid, enters having 'just spent a pleasant afternoon at the cinema' and announces that she found the dinner guests Mr and Mrs Martin waiting at the door. The Smiths have in fact eaten dinner and go off to dress for it. Mary shows in the Martins who behave as if they were complete strangers, who once met travelling third class on the same train from Manchester to London. In a long logical argument they discover that they are man and wife, while Mary, in an equally logical speech, proves that they are not and leaves, telling us that her real name is Sherlock Holmes. The Smiths return and an embarrassed silence ensues which leads into another odd conversation about a ring at the door which they discuss until Mr Smith finally opens it to reveal the Captain of the Fire Brigade, who helps to settle the argument, but is disappointed to find that there are no fires ('Not even a wee little beginning of a fire') to put out. He offers to tell them stories of his experiences, and a series of 'fables' follows until Mary discovers that she and the Captain are in some way acquainted. Mary then recites a poem and is pushed out. The Captain leaves and the two married couples sink conversationally into nonsense, leaving the play to end with the dialogue with which it began spoken by Mr and Mrs Martin (or, if so desired, once more by Mr and Mrs Smith). After the first of the Fire Chief's 'fables' Mrs Martin asks what the moral is to which he replies: 'It's for you to discover it.' This could be taken, mockingly, as the subject of the play that establishes the characteristics of Ionesco's work: simple plot, dehumanized characters and absurd (if logically so) language. It was an attack on cliché in life and language, but the tragedy produced laughter in the theatre, and in his subsequent work Ionesco has recognized the arbitrary nature of dramatic labels:

> I have called my comedies 'anti-plays', 'comical dramas', and my dramas 'pseudo-dramas', or 'tragical farces', for, it seems to me, the comical is tragic, and the tragedy of man, derisory. For the modern critical spirit nothing can be taken entirely seriously, nor entirely lightly.
>
> ('Discovering the Theatre', p. 86)

The definition of tragedy and comedy has never been easy, and there has been a recent tendency exemplified by George Steiner's book *The Death of Tragedy* (1961), to doubt whether the former is still possible. The so-called 'black comedy' which we greet with uncertain laughter, is an attempt to fill the hiatus. Ronald Peacock's simple axiom that drama must be one of two things, either comic or intensely moving (*The Art of Drama*, London 1957, p. 189) will no longer do, if indeed it ever was adequate. J. L. Styan, in his study of what he calls 'Dark Comedy', produces a long list of distinguished antecedents to this 'contemporary' solution – including Euripides, Marlowe, Shakespeare, and Molière – and he reminds us that the best comedy 'teases and troubles' its audience, and can be painful. Twentieth-century dramatists have available a large number of forms and varieties of stage on which to put them, but Absurd drama, whatever its form or method of staging, is usually very funny and very terrifying, pushing the spectator forward, then muddling him, compelling a personal assessment of his response and offering opposites which flourish in his mind:

> Affairs in dark comedy rarely conclude: they persist, and their repercussions may be felt to be unlimited. This drama does not make decisions for us, but at most suggests likelihoods, depicts chanciness and stresses both sides. It stimulates by implications, and it does not pass judgements ...
>
> (Styan, pp. 251, 278)

All of which could as well be applied to Brecht as Ionesco! If the academic critic wishes to separate comedy and tragedy, for the sake of convenience, the pleasure (and pain) for a contemporary audience comes from watching the playwright keep his balance on a tight-rope.

Ionesco is not committed to artistic definitions, nor to political or religious codes; but neither can his plays be mere entertainment. In *Improvisation* (1956) he illustrates the dilemma by parodying both attitudes: that of the conservative critic who believes that theatre serves no purpose beyond amusing an audience, and that of the socially-orientated critic who believes that the theatre must be didactic. There is no more telling image in all Ionesco's plays than that of the *cité radieuse* at the opening of *The Killer*: a world where all social problems have been eliminated, yet where death still renders life futile and absurd, for, in the total condition of human illusion, two facts emerge: death and anguish (see Raymond Williams, *Modern Tragedy*, pp. 152–3) and the only authentic society must be based, according to Ionesco, on this common anguish. It is this which gives universality to the fundamental and private obsessions of Ionesco. The result is both thematic and technical:

> If our world is one in which people strike us as inhuman, then let us place robots on the stage. If we feel that the physical aspects of life deny us the full development of our spiritual potential, then by all means let that be reflected in a play whose décor or properties slowly dominate the characters. If language is worn out, then let us show the solidified forms of that language as cliché and slogan, or words reduced to pure agglomerates of sound.
>
> (Pronko, *Ionesco*, p. 13)

This can be illustrated by *The Chairs* (1952). An old man and woman have lived a mediocre life on an island. The old man is convinced that he has something important to say before he dies and, encouraged by his wife, he invites all remaining human beings to come and hear the message. A chair is brought for each guest (who is invisible) and when they are all assembled the old couple leap to their deaths in the sea, leaving the Orator (the only other visible character) to deliver the message. But he is a mute and can only grunt (for what important message can be communicated and who could sum up life in a sentence?) The Orator leaves, and for a long time we watch the stage, full of chairs, listening to the waves washing on the walls of the house. Although the text includes an episode with a blackboard, this was not used in the first production; Ionesco intended a purely visual and aural conclusion.

Such a play brings us to the second period in Ionesco's career. Hitherto he has been mainly concerned with language, which, as Coe remarks, he has raised to the status of an object-in-itself. His characters serve as vehicles for this and could, in some places, be replaced by a tape recorder (Coe, *Ionesco*, pp. 43–4). Henceforth up to *The Killer* (1957) Ionesco is concerned more with the proliferation of objects. In this he fulfils the dictum of Artaud that the stage is a place to be filled (with dead objects now, not the fossils of language) and parodies the theatrical tradition of Zola and his followers (who, in their quest for naturalism, flooded the stage with the objects of everyday living); he also, as Guicharnaud points out, replaces the qualitative image of Sartre's nausea with a quantitative one (*Modern French Theatre*, p. 183). Thus, in *The New Tenant* (1953), a victim of duty (the subject of the preceding play in 1952) is gradually submerged beneath a clutter of furniture which reminds us how we, too, are often buried beneath familiar habits and, like the New Tenant, might as well ask the furniture removers to turn off the light and leave us to relax into a living death.

By 1957, with *The Killer*, Ionesco seemed to be taking a new line. His hero Berenger reminds us of Camus's absurd hero (Ionesco is an ardent admirer of Camus). Ionesco rejects political commitment, but he is committed: existence is the first of all commitments, and the rest are incidental. He is passionately concerned with man's freedom, and in *Rhinoceros* (1959) illustrates this by contrasting Berenger with Jean, a man organized around slogans and fixed ideas. Berenger, keenly aware of the meaninglessness of every day existence, seeks a kind of oblivion in alcohol until the end of the play when he achieves (or is forced into) a more heroic position. Jean has blind strength, like a rhinoceros, and argument is impossible with him. By the end of the play Berenger is left alone surrounded by a herd of these thick-skinned rhinos. A shocking but amusing image, creating power and violence in the theatre. And perhaps something more, for Coe has pointed out that Ionesco's experience is fundamentally Nazi, and that the rhinos are specifically a denunciation of Nazi ideology, a world where social order is based on logic (and therefore without meaning), where the civil authorities (it is never the military) are menacing and evil. As for politics, since they too are presumably based on reason, they are obviously inadequate for the solution of problems in an irrational world (see Coe, *Ionesco*, pp. 89 ff.).

Perhaps also Ionesco has reached an impasse. The last Berenger play, *Exit the King* (1962), with its mythic content, has been followed by silence.

Ionesco, then, is concerned with the deadly nature of bourgeois life, its mechanical quality and the loss of a sense of mystery, the loneliness of individuals and their difficulties in communicating in a language also deadened by habit. Unlike the tramps and outcasts of Beckett and Adamov, Ionesco's characters are lonely in what *ought* to be a community context; and unlike Beckett, Ionesco seems to have moved from the very absurd and dehumanized play to the more sympathetic and human kind of play in which, perhaps, Mrs Martin could find a moral.

BECKETT

If *The Bald Prima Donna* was the earlier play, it was Beckett's *Waiting for Godot* (1953) that made the themes and method acces-

sible on a world-wide scale. As Esslin has shown in his excellen
chapter on Beckett, the play had an enormous success in France
has been translated into more than twenty languages and per
formed in at least twenty-two countries (including Ireland). If w
add to these statistics details such as that the first performance o
Endgame (in French) was at the Royal Court Theatre in 1957
that *Happy Days* opened at the Cherry Lane Theatre (New York
in 1961, and that *Play* was first performed (in German) at Ulm ir
1963, we can gain some idea of the size of audience that Becket
has reached. Considering the enigmatic and pessimistic nature o
his plays, this popular acceptance is surprising.

It is common knowledge that Beckett was associated with Jame:
Joyce, has chosen to live in France and write in French, and presents in his literature a pessimism apparently unrelated to his actua
life in which he is the most balanced and serene of men. More thar
any other dramatist of this 'school', Beckett dispenses witl
plot. As Esslin remarks, *Waiting for Godot* does not tell a story
it explores a static situation: 'Nothing happens, nobody comes
nobody goes, it's awful.' Even the apparent differences betweer
Act I and Act II only serve to emphasize the essential sameness o:
the situation. The dialogue makes the customary use of music-hal
patter and mime, and the title introduces implications which canno
be dismissed as accidental. Since Beckett's care for language i:
notorious, he must deliberately have allowed a French nonsense
word, with its implications, to stand in the English translation, and
therefore the suggestion of God-ot is as permissible as is the suggestion that the word could refer to Godeau, the racing cyclist,
echo Simone Weil's *Attente de Dieu* and contain, as Eric Bentley
has suggested, an allusion to Balzac's comedy *Le Faiseur*, usually
known as *Mercadet*, after the speculator who explains his financial
difficulties by blaming them on his former partner Godeau, who
absconded with their joint capital and who does return at the end o:
the play with a huge fortune which, miraculously, saves the situa-

tion. The story of the two thieves appears early in the play; these two malefactors happened to be present at a unique opportunity for salvation – one of them happened to make a hostile remark and was damned, the other happened to contradict him and was saved. Chance exclamations damn or save, and this is matched by the unpredictability of Godot as reported by the boy (or boys?). Hope of salvation is a *subject* of the play, but Esslin asks, does this mean that it is a Christian play? May not this very hope of salvation which we find in the play be an act of Bad Faith, a refusal on our part to face the reality, that there is no Godot, and by believing that there is, to avoid our responsibilities by simply waiting (Esslin pp. 52 ff.)?

In *Waiting for Godot* two characters pass the time waiting by playing games on the open road. In his second play *Endgame* two characters play the final game shut up in a room. Here a blind old man, Hamm, sits in a wheelchair (he cannot stand) waited on by his servant Clov (who cannot sit down); in the room also, in dust-bins, are Hamm's legless parents Nagg and Nell. The world out-side is dead, or at least these four people believe they are the last survivors of the race after some great catastrophe. Although Clov hates Hamm, he must obey his orders, and the basic question of the play (its plot, one might say) is whether or not Clov will muster enough will-power to leave Hamm, who will then die (but so will Clov – and since supplies have run out the question is irre-levant!). Like *Waiting for Godot* this play has been variously interpreted, even as a biographical treatment embodying the relationship between Joyce and Beckett. The sense of deadness is remarkably consistent, lightened only by the possible vision of a small boy who has been, for some reason, given less prominence in the English translation. In the French version this little boy, a 'potential creator' contemplates his navel, 'that is, he fixed his attention on the great emptiness of Nirvana, nothingness, of which Democritus the Abderite has said, in one of Beckett's favourite quotations, "Nothing is more real than nothing"' (Esslin, p. 72).

Both these plays show a lack of plot and also, in the conventional sense, of character, for character presumes that personality matters, just as plot assumes that events in time have significance – and both these postulates are questioned in the plays. In his subsequent plays for stage and radio, Beckett does not probe quite so deeply, but the themes persist: the difficulty of finding meaning in a world subject to incessant change, and the limitations of language as a means of arriving at or communicating valid truths. Pronko has pointed out that stichomythia, so dynamic as a means of interchange in Corneille, suggests here a lack of communication – each man following his own thoughts, while the silences and pauses isolate words and phrases and the repetitions remind us how monotonous, repetitive and tedious life is (Pronko, *Avant-Garde*, p. 57).

Yet, if Beckett devalues language, he continues to use it and, bilingually, to show a mastery of it. With such success, moreover, that Bamber Gascoigne, discussing twentieth-century poetic drama, concludes that it turns out to be written in prose: *Waiting for Godot* (*Twentieth Century Drama*, p. 68). For want of a better tool language has been moulded into an instrument for naming the unnameable, and Esslin concludes that this recognition of absurdity is once more the starting-point of exhilaration and freedom: 'For to know nothing is nothing, not to want to know anything likewise, but to be beyond knowing anything, that is when peace enters, to the soul of the incurious seeker' (Esslin, p. 87). It might, for most of us, however, be the peace that passeth all understanding, were it not for the central paradox of Beckett's work.

For most of us Beckett is, simply, the author of *Waiting for Godot*, and it comes as a surprise to find that his critics treat the plays almost as a footnote to his major work the novels. *Murphy* was published in 1938 (that significant year again!) and when

Beckett left for the Unoccupied Zone of France in 1942 he started writing *Watt*, published in 1953. While he was writing *Waiting for Godot* (1947–9) he was also working on a trilogy, *Molloy* and *Malone Dies* (published in 1951) and *The Unnameable* (published in 1953), followed by *How It Is* in 1961. Looking at this mass of writing the main impression is that the spontaneity and fantasy which inspired Ionesco are here replaced by a mind that deliberately excludes those qualities. One of Beckett's rare utterances (and unlike Ionesco, Beckett has consistently refused to explain or talk about his work) consists of three dialogues discussing modern painters in the first of which he describes a new form of art which he would prefer:

> The expression that there is nothing to express, nothing with which to express, nothing from which to express, no power to express, no desire to express, together with the obligation to express.
> (The three dialogues are reprinted in *Beckett*, Twentieth Century Views, pp. 16–22.)

The art Beckett objects to reflects those bourgeois values in which he can no longer believe. For Beckett, as for Ionesco, science and philosophy have produced a void, and, given Nothing as the universal ultimate, what significance can art have unless we can find one that can satisfactorily express nothing?

Beckett's first hero (and subsequent heroes reflect him) takes his name Belacqua from the lute-maker of Florence and friend of Dante found on that lonely plain where souls wait lost to this world, but not yet ready to enter purgatory: a place of blankness, indolence and indecision. *More Kicks than Pricks* (1934) traces, in ten short stories, the career of this Belacqua Shuah through three marriages to his accidental death and solemn burial. This is a hero for whom idleness is a positive statement of existence, and the heroes that follow subscribe to the basic maxim – taught by the Sicilian rhetorician, Gorgias of Lentini (483–375 B.C.) – that nothing has any real existence, and that if anything real did exist it

F

could not be known, and that if anything were to exist and be known it could not be expressed in speech. Critics (such as F. J Hoffman in *Samuel Beckett: The Language of Self* (1962)) who trace Beckett's inheritance from literature rather than philosophy and see his hero evolving out of Dostoevsky and Kafka – for example Gregor Samsa in Kafka's tale 'Metamorphosis' who literally shrinks into an insect *becoming* what he fears he is – arrive at the same conclusion. Dostoevky's Underground Man (the hero of *Notes from the Underground*, 1864) becomes Kafka's insect, becomes, finally, the non-hero of Beckett. But, and here is the paradox, all Beckett's heroes, writing about self-definition, 'invoke a language of careful and even arduous enquiry; they are precise almost beyond the decent limits of precision' (see Hoffman Chapters 1 and 2). It is this rational mind which is as much a cause of obscurity as the meaninglessness of the world since the heroes insist upon acting as logical beings, although logic must show them the absurdity of such behaviour. In this Beckett differ from Ionesco, who exploits the surface absurdities, and Joyce who gloried in language and erudition. Beckett rejects learning and sees language as part of the failure to know where or what we are, an impenetrable barrier (see Coe, *Beckett*, pp. 10–12). Thus Beckett's heroes not only deny that they are philosophers, they positively flaunt an ignorance of philosophy and yet remain perpetually concerned with questions that have been problems since pre-Socratic times: the nature of Self, the world, and God. Moreover, by divorcing these heroes from social situations, Beckett can never force them, as the heroes of Camus and Sartre are forced to a moment of decision so that we have the distinct impression, in the words of R. N. Coe, that Beckett's people have collapsed under the burden of choice, responsibility and anguish, that an existentialist world, which they take for granted, exposes them to (Coe pp. 73 ff). Molloy, Moran, Malone and *The Unnameable* are all monologues leading finally to *How It Is*, where the thinker, gasp

ng in the mud, moves slowly at intervals, dragging his sack of
ardine tins, occasionally bumping into another Pim or Pom (or
s it Bim or Bom?), forcing out nostalgic memories of life in the
ight.

The one undeniable influence on Beckett – beginning in 1931
with the publication of an essay – was Proust, whose work reveals
hose themes which pre-occupy Beckett: the tyrannies of time and
anguage which hinder an awareness of self: 'How am "I", an a-
emporal being imprisoned in time and space, to escape from my
mprisonment, when I *know* that outside time and space lies Noth-
ng, and that "I", in the ultimate depths of my reality, am Nothing
lso?' (Coe, p. 18). This question leads to others found in Proust –
he discontinuity of personality, the necessary solitude of the artist
nd the belief that suffering is the one force powerful enough to
stablish the identity of Self. But, again, some questions cannot
be even formulated, and these are the questions Beckett begins to
ry and ask in *Murphy*, questions we must fumblingly express as:
what am I, what are time and space, mind and matter? Beckett's
heroes are determined to answer these questions and not by taking
efuge in mysticism. This insistence on rationalism sets Beckett
part from the Absurdists. As Coe puts it: '"the Absurd" is a
nethod which proceeds, by means of annihilation of rational con-
epts, to a point where the ultimate reality, irrational by definition,
nay be glimpsed through the wreckage. But Beckett, by contrast,
herishes rationality above all things, but drives it to the point at
which . . . reason itself is transmuted into the still vaster reality of
he irrational' (Coe, p. 20).

Thus when Arsene, in *Watt*, is handing over the job of looking
fter Mr Knott, he gives the hero the benefit of his experience (in
twenty-eight-page-long paragraph!), and the significant point of
his experience was the Change. This Change is an awareness of
omething other than Roquentin's nausea, for that awareness of the
Absurd demonstrates the invalidity of rationalism. The Change is

an awareness that man can never escape rationality, and involves man in a logical contradiction which is impossible even when it exists, and which Beckett sums up in a joke he patriotically shifts from Ireland to Wales: Do not comes down the ladder, Ifor, I ha' taken it away. The ladder properly belongs to the philosophe' Wittgenstein, and what Beckett means here is that one can only affirm that meaning does not exist in terms which *imply* that it does. Nothing, therefore, implies Something, but this as we know is impossible: *ex nihilo nihil fit*. The concept of Nothing, therefore whether we think of it, speak of it, or write about it, destroys itself because it produces Something: the ladder of affirmations canno' exist and yet one has to climb down it. How? Beckett's solution could be science but is, in fact, mathematics. Even when his heroes cannot see or speak they can usually count. In mathematics numbers *exist* because they function in relation to others, but we have no way of proving their existence, or indeed of defining them precisely. As Hugh Kenner points out, 'somewhere between $1\frac{16}{40}$ and $1\frac{70}{169}$ we may expect $\sqrt{2}$ to exist, though we should no' expect to find it. But we can name it, know it is there, although it is impossible' (Hugh Kenner, *Samuel Beckett: A Critical Study* New York, 1961, p. 107).

Given the pre-occupations of Beckett, a move into the theatre was almost inevitable, for the spoken word approximates the instantaneous present more than the written, and if the novels are from one point of view, a search for the tense in which past and future dissolve into 'now' the form of a play resolves this problem (Coe, p. 88). The essential difference in a play is that the character has to be physically there, even if still extremely passive (particularly for an existential hero). Alain Robbe-Grillet records his surprise at actually seeing a Beckett hero, and realizing what this physical presence actually means. He sees the two tramps as being on the stage, but with a difference:

A character in a play usually does no more than *play a part*, as all of those about us do who are trying to shirk their own existence. But in Beckett's play it is as if the two tramps were on the stage without a part to play.

They are there; so they must explain themselves. But they do not seem to have the support of a prepared and carefully learned text. They must invent. They are free.

Of course their freedom is not put to any use. Just as there is nothing for them to recite, so there is nothing for them to invent, either, and their conversation, which has no continuous thread to sustain it, is reduced to absurd fragments: automatic exchanges, word-play, mock arguments all more or less abortive. They try everything, at random. The only thing they are not free to do is go away, cease to be there: they have to stay because they are waiting for Godot.

('Samuel Beckett, or "Presence" in the Theatre', *Beckett*, Twentieth Century Views, p. 113).

This action (?) of waiting is reflected in the dialogue which can be recognized as the absurd efforts of a Sisyphus who remains a prisoner of the endless fictions he produces. And it is an ambiguous action. Waiting may be heroic (in that to wait implies that a personality has been maintained long enough for waiting to be possible, which, in our present condition is heroic) or it may be something worse than foolish, a linguistic illusion. Like the plays, the argument for waiting is circular: we are, therefore we wait, therefore we wait *for* something, therefore we are. Thus 'Godot' may be nothing but a name for a life which pointlessly misinterprets itself and the language by which it expresses that falsification (see Gunther Anders, 'Being Without Time: On Beckett's Play "Waiting for Godot"', *Beckett*, Twentieth Century Views, p. 143). Merely because Beckett's characters *are*, they wait, and commentators often borrow Heidegger's term 'Geworfenheit' to describe this. But Beckett's heroes are not as heroic as that; the fact that they have been 'thrown into' the world is not, for them, a beginning of action or decision. They champion the theory that even in a meaningless situation life must have a meaning. Beckett presents an inability in man to be nihilist, not nihilism.

Yet these fools 'looking, with inadequate strength, on a wrong road, for a goal that perhaps does not exist' (Wellershof, 'Failure of an attempt at De-Mythologisation', *Beckett*, Twentieth Century Views, p. 107), compel compassion. The tone, at least in his early writing, is one of farce, and we do not mean the chamberpot or bedroom comedy. Farce as a vehicle that contains all human sadness allows us to feel with and for Beckett's clowns even as they are detached from us. In much of Beckett's work the tone means more than meaning, and it is this warmth which denies the metaphysician the last word, and qualifies Absurdity.

GENET

Nothing could more illustrate the Frenchness of the situation than the fact that President Auriol, on the intercession of Jean Cocteau and Jean-Paul Sartre, granted, in 1948, a free pardon for all Genet's crimes because the crime for which he had been then sentenced had been committed by someone else *and* because his literary work – 'of a very great poet' – had freed him from the evil and crime which had characterized his early life. This illegitimate homosexual thief began writing, in prison, a series of prose poems, or novels: *Our Lady of the Flowers* (1944, but dated 1942, Prison de Fresnes), *Miracle of the Rose* (1945), *Pompes Funèbres* (1947), *Querelle of Brest* (1947), and *The Thief's Journal* (1948?) – all, except *Pompes Funèbres*, now available in English translated by Bernard Frechtman (*Querelle of Brest* by Gregory Streatham). The dates are far from reliable, for Genet has experienced difficulties in publication not merely because he was in prison, but also because he tends towards what society often calls obscenity. In 1947 he wrote his first play *Deathwatch*, which portrays the tensions felt by three men in a prison cell dominated by the distant presence of a Negro murderer called Snowball. This was followed by *The Maids* (original version acted in 1946), *The Balcony* (1957), *The Blacks* (1959), and *The Screens* (1961). John Russell Taylor ends his entry on Genet in the Penguin Dictionary by saying that, although claimed for both the Theatre of the Absurd and the Theatre of Cruelty, Genet is essentially 'an original, making his own solitary, but unpredictable way through modern French drama.'

Certainly Esslin's claim, in Chapter 4, is more tentative than usual for this latest of a long line of *poètes maudits* stretching from Villon, through de Sade, Verlaine and Rimbaud. Esslin seizes upon an image drawn from *The Thief's Journal* of a man caught in a Hall of Mirrors, 'trapped by his own distorted reflections, trying to find the way to make contact with the others he can see around him but being rudely stopped by barriers of glass' (Esslin, p. 195). Such an image exactly contains and connects isolation, the failure of communication, distortion of experience and, in its mirror effect, the existential situation. The method can be seen in *The Maids*. The scene is an elegant boudoir where a lady is being dressed by her maid whom she addresses as Claire. The lady is very haughty, the maid servile – but the ringing of an alarm clock dissolves the scene and we learn that both women, in fact, are maids, and that the one called Claire is Solange, while the 'lady' is called Claire. The two maids have just caused the arrest of their mistress's lover by sending an anonymous letter to the police, and when the telephone rings to announce his release they realize that their denunciation will be revealed so they plan to poison their mistress. When she arrives they serve her poisoned tea, but just as she is about to drink it she notices that the telephone receiver is off the hook and, in the confusion, news of her lover's release slips out and she leaves. The maids are left alone to resume their charade, and Claire insists on being served the tea (since she *plays* the lady) which she drinks to prove her courage – Solange has failed on a previous occasion to poison their mistress.

These two girls are linked together by the love-hatred of being each other's mirror image; but Genet's mirrors are more complex than this, for he wishes the women to be played by men.

Genet's revolt, then, is a ritual – the ritual of wish-fulfilment, an act wholly absurd since it mirrors its own futility. But in turning to the theatre Genet broke out of the daydream that viciously dominates his novels. His plays are based on fantasy and dreams, and discuss the impotence of individuals trapped in society, trying to find a meaning through the methods of myth and ritual, but doomed to failure, for, as the revolutionaries in *The Balcony* show, when men have destroyed one myth, another has to be created equally spurious. But the fantasy on the stage is brutal and disturbing, simply because an audience exists collectively and not as solitary individuals. Esslin finds in Genet's plays psychological truth, social protest, and the hallmarks of Absurd drama – the abandonment of character and motivation in favour of states of mind, devaluation of language as a means of communication, the rejection of didactic purpose and the theme of alienation, solitude and the search for meaning (Esslin, p. 228). But Genet is not easy to define, even when the definition is attempted by Jean-Paul Sartre in his monumental study, *Saint Genet: Actor and Martyr* (1952). Sartre is concerned to find in Genet an instance of Existential Man, one who consciously, within a given situation, chooses his own self and acts out the consequences. Yet Sartre finds Genet is not an Absurdist; whereas honest minds can no longer be sensitive to anything but absurdity, others cherish a deep conviction that life must have a meaning: 'The more horrible their situation, the tighter their grip. The more absurd the world is today, the more necessary it is to hold out until tomorrow. Tomorrow, dawn will break. The present darkness is warrant of the fact. Genet is one of them' (*Saint Genet*, p. 49). Later in his study, Sartre returns to this difference, describing Camus's discovery of Absurdity but pointing out that Genet is at the opposite pole: 'if Genet is astounded by the course of the world, it is precisely because events seem to him to have a meaning' (*Saint Genet*, p. 255).

Admitting that Genet does display techniques and themes which invite the label, it is also true that reality keeps breaking through to offer a more 'conventional type of theatrical experience in addition to the avant-garde challenge' (Thody, *Jean Genet*, p. 49). Moreover, such a label obscures Genet's political significance (his last two plays have been concerned with race problems and the Algerian grievances against France) which producers, encouraged by Genet's own attitude, have failed to bring out. The fact that he is so unremittingly pessimistic in things political should not, Philip Thody rightly observes, blind us from seeing in his plays, how society is evolving (p. 195). This kind of qualification is extensively carried out by R. N. Coe in his study *The Vision of Jean Genet* (1968). Coe's study is complex, philosophical and, for this reader, less persuasive in this instance than his writings on Ionesco and Beckett. He points out that Genet's concept of the independent voices of objects does link him with Camus, Ionesco and the 'Pataphysicians, and plunges him into the paradoxes of the Absurd situation; but Genet arrives there by developing his own first principles. There are hardly any traces of specifically Absurdist influences in the novels or even the dramas until *The Screens*, and yet pages of *The Thief's Journal* which develop this vision are 'among the classic documents in any history of the Absurd' (Coe, p. 144). In so far as *The Maids* and *The Blacks* use the techniques of the circus and music hall as found in Ionesco and other *avant-garde* dramatists, they could be classed as Absurd plays, but to do so involves a contradiction since Genet is concerned not with denying the significance of human experience, but with trying to discover new dimensions of meaning in it (Coe, p. 213). The profane world may reveal itself as gratuitous and the mystical world is unfathomable, but where the two worlds meet poetry is created, and in Genet's drama we have a collision between a drama which sees everyday things from outside and a drama which strives to create a perfect illusion (and thus loses contact with that profane world on which it is based):

> The first is the world of the Absurd, the gratuitous, where no miracles are possible; the second is the world of the *true* miracle, the province of angels, perhaps, but not of poets. And in between the two ... lies the domain of the false miracle ... (Coe, p. 124)

In exploring this dualism Coe comes to the conclusion that a vision of life 'as a ritualistic tragedy whose symbolism creates a higher meaning for death, and so redeems existence from absurdity, permeates every page that Genet has written' (Coe, p. 218).

By their conciseness the two early plays appear to have been modelled upon and inspired by Sartre's *Huis Clos*, but the later plays are nearer Brechtian epic in technique and they are committed plays. In fact, Genet appears to have become *engagé* in spite of himself, because what he is doing and what the audience does are in conflict. Genet abstracts his heroes from a social context to show them as negative characters, concerned only with some kind of transcendental absolute, but the audience puts them back where they came from and interprets them as positive heroes or victims in a social or political setting, because a negative hero may become positive in a social context and that is what the theatre almost inevitably provides. Thus Genet's dilemma is that, in refusing to create a socialist theatre, he produces a negative revolt that must be interpreted as social (Coe, p. 256). For Coe, therefore, the last three plays transform Artaud's Theatre of Cruelty (to which Genet came late and, finding a correspondence, retrospectively adopted Artaud's principles) and Brecht's Theatre of Provocation into a highly disquieting Theatre of Hatred.

However Artaud's influence worked, its effect is strongly felt, so much so that Brustein sees in Genet's drama the only realization of Artaud's ideas. Artaud, he believes, would have found

Ionesco too frivolous and Beckett too nihilistic, lacking in the delirious quality Artaud envisioned in the theatre (*The Theatre of Revolt*, p. 377; see also Charles Marowitz, 'The Revenge of Jean Genet', *The Encore Reader*, pp. 170–8). In Genet Brustein finds this delirious quality, and perhaps this is what Joseph McMahon means when he describes a theatre audience finding that it has been invited to assist at a Black Mass, instead of the conventional ceremonies of innocence the theatre's illusions usually present, and feeling some disturbance on recognizing that the blasphemy has been organized because they wanted to participate in it anyway (J. H. McMahon, *The Imagination of Jean Genet*, Yale, 1963, p. 133).

8

Limitations

The first, and least important, limitation is probably the explicit nature of the term 'Absurd', already hinted at in Pronko's objection to it as to a label like 'The School of Paris'. His insistence upon the label *'avant-garde'* stems from the difficulty of fitting in certain relevant dramatists under even so capacious an umbrella as 'Absurd': the work of Ghelderode (1918–37, since when he has produced virtually nothing) or Pichette (whose work is often so surrealist that it could not be produced, merely printed) is less important than that of their successor Schehadé, whose dramatic world has wonder and innocence antagonistic to the worlds of Beckett or Ionesco, suggesting that 'life is more than mere appearance, that it may be for everyone, as it is for his heroes, a constant if desperate search for truth, for innocence, for youth, and for the ideal' (Pronko, *Avant-Garde*, p. 196). Such a dramatist, clearly, cannot be called Absurd, yet with those dramatists we can call Absurd he shares a common determination to attack naturalism and realism in the theatre, using some kind of spectacle from the non-literary theatre. In both the use of concrete objects replaces words as a means of communication leading to a new kind of drama, where neither comedy nor tragedy alone can achieve the required and bitter lucidity. It is capricious to isolate Absurd drama from the general adventure in contemporary theatre, where common methods seek to revitalize and save it from a stagnation imposed upon it by over sixty years of naturalism and thesis play.

But we are at this point reminded of a more crucial limitation in this kind of revolt, inherent in the fabric of Absurd drama itself, and superbly illustrated by Adamov. The omission of Adamov from the preceding discussion was strategic. Esslin, in Chapter 2 of *The Theatre of the Absurd*, opens his discussion with the frank statement that the author of some of the most powerful plays in that theatre now rejects all the work that might be classified under that heading. Adamov thus provides an interesting example of a dramatist who, in the forties, could not be persuaded to use a real name in his plays, and who, in the sixties, writes a full-scale historical drama of the Paris Commune of 1871.

Adamov, born in Russia, educated in Switzerland and Germany, came to Paris in 1924 at the age of sixteen and began writing Surrealist poetry. During the 1930s he withdrew from literature and underwent some kind of spiritual crisis described in *L'Aveu (The Confession)* the first section of which he published in the significant year of 1938. It is, in Esslin's words, a 'brilliant statement of the metaphysical anguish that forms the basis of existentialist literature and of the Theatre of the Absurd' (Esslin, p. 89). Long before writing his first play, Adamov had documented a whole philosophy of the Absurd. This changes because Adamov, like Camus and Sartre, was in France during the Second World War, so that by 1946 he was giving a very personal kind of support to the Communist Party. About 1945 he wrote his first play *La Parodie* in which he deliberately avoids subtleties of plot, characterization and language, producing a theatre of gesture. The problems of communication continue to obsess him in his next play *L'Invasion* written shortly afterwards, but in *Professor Taranne* (1951) – a literal transcription of a dream – he begins to move out towards a more realistic world and combine in one character affirmative and negative attitudes. Taranne, in asserting his worth as a citizen and scholar, exposes his claims as fraudulent but 'it is by no means clear whether the play is meant to show a fraud unmasked, or an innocent man confronted by a monstrous conspiracy of circumstances engineered to destroy his claims'

(Esslin, p. 106). This outward movement culminates in *Le Ping-Pong*, a play about life and the futility of human endeavour: 'But while *La Parodie* merely asserted that whatever you do, in the end you die, *Le Ping-Pong* provides a powerful and closely integrated argument to back that proposition – it also shows how so much of human endeavour becomes futile, and *why*' (Esslin, p. 110).

By 1955 Adamov was working on *Paolo Paoli*, in which he examines the 'why' of the First World War and begins to abandon Absurd techniques in favour of Brechtian epic theatre. Having freed himself of his own obsessions, he is at liberty to experiment with models outside his own experience. Esslin regrets the loss of 'the fine frenzy, the haunting power of neurosis that gave the earlier plays their magnetic, poetical impact' (Esslin, p. 117), but it could be objected that Adamov, even in the early plays, has seldom if ever involved our emotions, only our intellect.

This conversion meets, at least, with Tynan's approval, and to his mind gets the priorities exactly right: 'he (Adamov) has thus espoused Marxism, not in order to make men equally happy, but to allow them to contemplate their condition on equal terms: "When the material obstacles are overcome, when man will no longer be able to deceive himself as to the nature of his unhappiness, then there will arise an anxiety all the more powerful, all the more fruitful, for being stripped of anything that might have hindered its realization"' (*Tynan on Theatre*, p. 191). But it is only fair to add that, if Absurd drama has to wait for these conditions, there is little likelihood that it will ever get written, and possibly Tynan knows this. In fact, Adamov's conversion is less surprising than if it had not happened. Grossvogel, discussing existentialism as a source for drama, suggests that at first glance it would appear to offer an auspicious area for development, concentrating as it does on choice performed by a hero who is 'bound neither by truth nor by good, but generating both – good being equated with the loftiest surge of freedom' (Grossvogel, p. 126).

In fact, as we have seen, Absurdity has its own built-in obsolescence. The thorough-going nature of its revolt (and it is much more thorough-going than previous revolutionary movements, such as those of Ibsen and Strindberg) ensures that it must be either a *terminus ad quem* or a *terminus ab quo*. Robert Corrigan has pointed out that, if a logically motivated hero and well-knit plot give meaning – spurious, illusory, and distorted – to the act which *exists* – alone and absurd – and rob it of its elemental importance which is simply absurdity, such absurdity is ill-suited to the extensiveness of literature, be it novel or drama. Making *situation* into the source of Absurd drama is exciting because dramatic situation is the essence of theatre, but it is also seriously limiting, and it is no accident that most Absurd dramas tend to be written in one act (Corrigan, Introduction to *Theatre in the Twentieth Century*).

Nor can it be simply a matter of technique, since the technique is suited to the subject and, as we have seen in discussing the novels *Nausea* and *The Outsider*, each has an air of finality about it. Descriptions of absurdity must lead, if mere repetition is to be avoided, to the questions 'how' and 'why' and even 'whence'. Adamov abandons it altogether, Genet's plays lengthen as commitment grows, Ionesco moves to a more human kind of drama; only Beckett (as we might expect) moves logically towards a silence that may ultimately be just that. Moreover, where theatre is concerned, some sort of plot is probably necessary. Obscurity in a poem is one thing (we can, after all, keep the poem and re-read it), but a single visit to the theatre must leave us with something to hold on to. In short, the theatre of Nothing, if it is to develop at all, will have to move to Something – whether the conventions and subjects are artistic, political, social, or religious.

There is one other possible limitation hinted at in calling these major dramatists 'The School of Paris', by which we hoped to emphasize that a group of exiles roughly based on that city made up the first wave of Absurd dramatists which has had to find its own solutions – in several cases an uneasy alliance with the Communist Party. A question remains: what influence such a movement has had and how *international* has that influence been? Esslin lists just over seventeen supposed parallels and proselytes, including some in Germany (where the Absurd struck a chord after the Second World War), some from behind the Iron Curtain (possibly reflecting Esslin's own predilections), and two in England, often mentioned in the same sentence, Harold Pinter and N. F. Simpson.

In his chapter on Pinter, John Russell Taylor asks where he should be placed and the answer is by himself (*Anger and After*, Chapter 7: an excellent treatment of Pinter's plays). Certainly Pinter is on record as admiring Beckett (primarily the novels, not the plays), and his plays do have a strong flavour of the Absurd about them, but noticeably Taylor deals adequately with his work without mentioning it. Existentialism depends upon individual feeling, and so we find even in The School of Paris widely differing responses. Moreover, the philosophical background natural to French drama is not natural to the British theatre. Pinter is certainly pre-occupied with Self – his basic question is: who or what am I? Certainly he is pre-occupied with the failures of language to communicate, the menaces of life (in his first play it is death, but this is later made less melodramatic) and its meaninglessness, and he uses rooms and furniture much in the way of Ionesco. But we do not immediately feel that the walls of those rooms are Camus's absurd walls – they suggest protection as well as isolation, and the failure to communicate stems less from the inability of language to do so and more from the unwillingness of people to expose themselves. As John Bowen puts it: 'Mr Pinter's buses really run; his observation may be appalled, but it is exact. His characters do not use language to show that language doesn't work; they use it as a cover for fear and loneliness' ('Accepting the Illusion',

Twentieth Century, February 1961, p. 162). Indeed, his language is an exact reproduction of natural speech with all the hesitations and repetitions – which, as Esslin points out, produces dialogue akin to the disintegrating language of the Absurd. Akin to, but different. The accumulated junk and rubbish of *The Caretaker* is pure Ionesco, but as R. N. Coe comments, if at first that play shows failure to communicate and the odd characters seem absurd, when Aston reveals that he has spent part of his life in a mental hospital, then nothing is surprising (Coe, *Ionesco*, p. 111). But this is not the whole story. Taylor describes Pinter's method as 'orchestrated' naturalism and it is a style which excludes cosmic disorders and grotesque fantasy of the kind we associate with Absurd Drama. No one in Pinter turns into a rhinoceros, but there are, in life, less obvious monsters. In his early plays, up to and including *The Caretaker*, Pinter was concerned with the problem of verification: was it possible to explain who the blind Negro was (in *The Room*), what crime, if any, Stanley had committed (in *The Birthday Party*), who the match-seller really was (in *A Slight Ache*) and what caused the tensions in the relationships between Goldberg and McCann or between the two gangsters in *The Dumb Waiter*? After *The Caretaker*, where the menace was immensely funny and very terrible, and, possibly because he had turned to television, Pinter widens out his room and introduces sex. From *Night School* to *The Homecoming* he explores the multiple possibilities of relationships with a woman, once more blending the humorous with the savage until this vein too seems exhausted, and he has turned, possibly influenced by his work in films, to the use of scenery as a reflection of emotional attitudes in *The Basement*, and, in *Landscape*, to a verbal creation of scenery. This reminds us that at first and throughout his career Pinter has been a distinguished poet of the theatre. We are still asking the question: who am I? But we are not asking it in particularly existential terms. Indeed, Pinter seems to have been least successful in those plays (e.g. *A Slight Ache* and *The Dwarfs*), where the presence of existential material is most probable, although in *The Homecoming* it has been so successfully assimilated that we can ignore it without missing the point of the play. Mr Esslin's summing up seems accurate, especially as it does not insist upon or point to an Absurd future for Pinter: his mastery of dialogue, accuracy of observation, originality, fertility, poetical vision, all these do indeed justify the highest hopes for his future development (Esslin, p. 292).

N. F. Simpson is altogether another matter. Although Wellwarth thinks highly of him (because of all British writers he seems to come closest in spirit to Jarry), it is doubtful whether he ought to be considered as an Absurd dramatist at all. John Russell Taylor complains that he looks parochial by comparison with Ionesco whom he seems to imitate, while Coe, admitting that he catches an echo of the lunacy of an Ionesco play, suggests that it is at an enormous cost. That which is not rational cannot be serious, and there stands *A Resounding Tinkle* to prove the point; in short Ionesco with 'the stuffing taken out' (Taylor, *Anger and After* p. 64; Coe, *Ionesco*, p. 111). Esslin sees him as an example of Absurd drama providing highly effective social comment but, in fact, the topicality of that comment seems, with other features, to put him with Osborne and Wesker, rather than with Beckett, Ionesco, and Pinter.

One could mention (although Esslin curiously does not) David Campton, whose *The Lunatic View* (1957) provided, in its subtitle, the phrase 'A Comedy of Menace', for Campton does indeed have a social conscience and defines the menace – which Pinter wisely leaves vague (thus each member of the audience can find a personal significance for it) – as the Bomb, and sees the Absurd theatre as a weapon against it (see Taylor, p. 165). It is not, however, a weapon Campton has used very much.

There is also, sadly neglected, James Saunders, whose play *Next Time I'll Sing to You* (1962) shows the influence of Ionesco and another personal use of the Absurd, for the play raises a crucial point of Existentialist philosophy: if Mason, the subject of the play, was really forgetting the world and forgotten by the world, and if no one was aware of his existence or his history, could he be said in any real sense of the term to exist? (Taylor, p. 183).

Noticeably with these dramatists the label 'Absurd' is not really needed. Particularly in the case of Pinter, it is best to treat him as standing on his own. The third wave is slightly different, and in many ways depressing, because it shows a vast number of playwrights imitating the Absurd for stage, television, and even cinema, in a rather mechanical way. We should mention, however, the remarkable and bewildering success of a play like Tom Stoppard's *Rosencrantz And Guildenstern Are Dead* (1967). This play, by a clever young dramatist, was staged at the National Theatre (whose dramaturge, Kenneth Tynan, has decided views on Absurd Theatre) and has been not merely popular, but also hailed critically as a masterpiece. Almost alone John Russell Taylor voiced the dilemma in judging this *three* act existential drama about two minor characters in *Hamlet* (the germ of the play rests on a misreading of the Court's greeting to these two) which was that it anthologized absurd features:

> If *Hay Fever*, *The Master Builder* and *Much Ado About Nothing* are usually your mark in the theatre, you will find *Rosencrantz And Guildenstern Are Dead* an intriguing and probably enjoyable experience. If you know your way round Beckett and early Pinter, not to mention a shoal of minor followers, you will be likely to find the road Rosencrantz and Guildenstern follow to dusty death all too familiar and uneventful to be worth travelling for a whole evening.
>
> (*Plays and Players*, June 1967. Taylor refers to the National Theatre production of *Much Ado About Nothing*, not to Shakespeare's play.)

America, too, seems not to have been congenial to Absurd drama, and Esslin explains this by suggesting that, after the

Second World War, America did not suffer the feeling of disillusionment characteristic of countries in Europe: the American
dream of the good life was still very strong. This is not entirely
plausible: American literature has, after all, been a long moral
dialogue in which the voices of pessimism have been at least as
strong as those of optimism. However, Esslin claims Albee for
Absurd Theatre, and once more we see a dramatist who shares
traits, but resists the label. Albee himself thinks that it is an unfortunate label from a movement that is over, but sees Absurd Theatre
as the Realistic Theatre of the present day 'facing as it does man's
condition as it is' and not pandering to the public need for self-
congratulation and reassurance by presenting 'false pictures of ourselves to ourselves' ('Which Theater is the Absurd One?' *Modern
American Theatre*, Twentieth Century Views, pp. 170–5). Which
is the kind of reasoning that brings Esslin to point out that
Pinter has always considered himself a much more ruthless realist
than the so-called social realists, for they water down the problem
by presupposing a solution, and focus attention on unessentials or
exaggerate their importance while leaving untouched the basic
problems of existence – loneliness, the mystery of the universe and
death (Esslin, p. 291).

Albee has shown himself, as Richard Duprey puts it, only a part-
time Absurdist, eclectic in his use of techniques and consistent only
in the pessimism behind all his plays. *Zoo Story* is absurd, but
The Death of Bessie Smith, although dealing with disillusionment,
is a piece of realism, and in *Who's Afraid of Virginia Woolf?*
Albee has adopted the conventions of the naturalistic stage
('Today's Dramatists', *American Theatre*, Stratford 10, pp. 209–
24). There is little sense in Albee that he feels he is living in an
Absurd universe – indeed much of his criticism is directed against
injustices that can be righted and he has shown, for example, in
Who's Afraid of Virginia Woolf? an almost sentimental desire to
make things turn out right. The question remains how useful the

label is; if, as Albee fears, it encourages 'non-think', then we had best meet Albee as Albee and not as an Absurd dramatist.

The other American candidate, Arthur Kopit, wrote *Oh Dad, Poor Dad, Mamma's Hung You in the Closet and I'm Feeling So Sad* (1960) while still an undergraduate at Harvard. It is a one-act situation which the dramatist has inflated. Esslin believes that beneath the parody there is a genuine concern (which has since expressed itself in *Indians* (1968)), but it is probably more accurate to suggest that Kopit, like Stoppard, has parodied the conventions of *avant-garde* drama in a play at once funny and not even mildly disturbing – and hence its popularity (see Wellwarth, p. 291). It is one of the problems of drama that an audience can cut any playwright down to its own size.

9
Objections

The limitations of Absurdity are, therefore, to a great extent inevitable. Once each artist has defined the condition, he must develop a response to the awareness, and once sufficient artists have done this the idea has passed into history. The usual progress is towards social criticism for, as Sartre recognized, his existential man is *in a situation* – and we usually call it society. And if the philosophical impetus weakens with time, it may also be true that it is characteristically French and, like good wine, does not travel well. If these are the practical limitations to Absurd art, can one produce objections to Absurdity as such? We have already seen Mr Tynan's perfectly legitimate preference, now shared by Adamov and Sartre among others: it is more appropriate to concentrate on removing problems capable of solution to clear the decks for the great problems which are, possibly, insoluble. The distinction appears more clear in theory than it often is. We have so many labels and patterns that it is difficult to feel they are useful. Is Absurdity useful? We do not ask at this stage if it is true, merely useful. David Tutaev, in an article, 'The Theatre of the Absurd . . . How Absurd?', having asked how far it *can* go (a chair playing to other chairs in an empty auditorium?) complains that it is nothing more than another romantic upsurge happening at a time when men's minds are most fissured. While Einstein, Planck, and Bohr destroyed the comfortable notions of causation, drama ignored events. It took the Russian revolution to drive drama into realism, and Hiroshima – the abdication of reason – to bring Absurd Theatre to the fore and show that man and his fate were merely a process of ever-changing and purposeless patterns. Technically such a theatre has made little or no impact in the use of space in the theatre, and it has failed to absorb the work of painters and sculptors as well as the discoveries of science. Thus, when man looks towards his future in the stars, the Absurd Theatre gives its audiences tales in the tradition of the Grand Guignol (*Gambit*, No. 2, London (n.d.), pp. 68–70).

Professor Coe has shown that Absurd Theatre has not ignored the discoveries of science, and for obvious reasons the theatre is slow to accommodate contemporary advances. In calling it Romantic, Tutaev possibly re-phrases Tynan's preference, but accuses the Absurd dramatist not of attending to the wrong things, but misusing imagination. Absurd fairy-tales strike Tutaev as inappropriate.

Because such a theatre has no obvious message with which to agree (or disagree), nor characters to love (or hate) and, as often as not tries to be as shocking as Ubu's first word, it invites in some a more forceful response than that of Tynan or Tutaev which, sometimes, looks suspiciously like bad temper. Joseph McMahon, for example, in his study of Genet, *The Imagination of Jean Genet* seems oddly unsympathetic to his subject, and complains of the 'assorted annoyances of the theatre of the absurd', the poverty of ideas and endless repetition hardly redeemed by the occasional dramatic invention which becomes self-destructive and, in its fascination with indecision, overlooks the large amount of decision-making necessary in the process of keeping body and soul together (McMahon, see pp. 8, 9, and 199). But no philosophy has ever insisted more than existentialism on the necessity for making decisions – existence is, after all, nothing else. It is possible that much of this argument springs from an unstated Christian point of view, which must feel objections to a body of ideas which assumes the death of God as one of its axioms. This kind of objection is not against the limiting nature of the art form or its conceptual basis but against Absurdity itself, and finds expression in Joseph Chiari's *Landmarks of Contemporary Drama* (1965).

Chiari's first point is that the notion of absurdity is untenable in a world where, statistically, more than half the population believes in a religion of some kind which ascribes order and purpose to life. This is a doubtful argument, raising the question not merely of what statistics show, but also what belief is, but it is a fact that more people feel, possibly vaguely, that life has a meaning than do not, though for many the notion could be described as either unthinking or Bad Faith. Chiari then takes a passage from Camus (a world that can be explained by reasoning, however faulty, etc. . . .) and comments, with some asperity, that faulty reasoning does not explain, it muddles – and he feels that the Absurdist argument is muddled. Man is an exile: exiled from what and by whom? A bad God? But this is to admit that there has been or is a God. In short, if the world is Absurd, it is man who thinks it so and has made it so. In this respect Sartre is wiser than most for, as Chiari points out, his absurdity is social, historical, and temporal, with nothing to it of the immanent or transcendent. Absurdity is, then, a relative not absolute notion, and one held by a minority.

Chiari distinguishes between the various *kinds* of Absurdity – that of Beckett which, like Kafka's, is in the imagination and recognizes that the human condition, deprived of God, faces hopelessness, and that of Ionesco and Adamov, which is fantastic and can decide what it pleases. Even Sartre is confused: granted that the world is absurd and that he must meet the ensuing freedom with a full sense of personal responsibility, it follows that Sartrian man *chooses* to be Sisyphus. Could he choose to be anything else? Not unless he can get rid of Absurdity, which he cannot do because even to entertain such a possibility would be Bad Faith. Beckett's world is meaningless because of the absence of Godot, but Ionesco's world is just plain incoherence, while Genet is concerned with individual identity, social ostracism, and theatre as ritual, but never Absurdity. The final annoyance is that the modern world insists that God is dead, but instead of enjoying the liberation worries about filling the void; and, moreover, if men cannot communicate, why bother to try and write plays (Chiari, chapters 1 and 3).

If Chiari's arguments (and they are fully and persuasively argued) do not convince, it is not because they have been anticipated by the accusation of Bad Faith, but because, like Sartre's nausea, they require agreement rather than compel it. Both points of view appeal on the same level, striking us as right or wrong according to the confirmation they offer to our own experience. We can summarize three possible objections to Absurdity:

1. It is simply not true. By this we mean not that the works of art fail to persuade us, but that we have a strong conviction that the world is not absurd. There is no reply to this; it is as much an act of faith as its opposite, and under these circumstances we are likely to treat Absurd plays like any other, preferring those from which virtues as we understand them can be drawn. Thus we shall be moved by compassion in *Waiting for Godot*, just as we admire Mother Courage – although in either case their creator might strongly disapprove.

2. Absurdity cannot at one and the same time be a tradition and a particular contemporary phenomenon. We feel uneasy that Esslin (and others) find Absurdity everywhere and yet claim for it a special contemporary importance. But this is an understandable, if confusing, critical procedure. Literature develops: something absolutely new does not happen, but parts of that development are more striking than others, and a latent sense of meaninglessness was given at a particular time a frightening relevance.

3. In spite of an honest conviction of Absurdity, plays and novels are written about it, and this in itself seems Bad Faith.

The importance of these objections must be left open. What has to be admitted (which is what Esslin in effect claims) is that a considerable body of literature exists which derives its inspiration from an existential view of life. Its aims are partly social, occasionally political, sometimes metaphysical, but at best always literary. If they work – in the theatre or the study – a beginning has been made, and such pragmatism will be helped by a sympathetic, but not necessarily convinced, understanding of what has been meant by Absurdity.

10

A Note on Novelists

The object of this short note is simple. The success of Mr Esslin's book has associated Absurdity and Drama in the popular mind to the exclusion of prose fiction, and, as we have seen, the first important works *Nausea* and *The Outsider* – not to mention Malraux, Kafka, and Dostoevsky – were novels. Thus, although no comprehensive study of the field of prose fiction and criticism can be made, some illustration is useful.

R. W. B. Lewis's study of novelists *The Picaresque Saint* was published in 1960 (i.e. pre-Esslin); in it he looks at a group of European and American novelists chosen as prophets or 'representative' men (the phrase is Emerson's and describes writers who give final expression to ideas that are only latent or partial in others). Lewis finds all these novelists, including Camus, under the shadow of Malraux and Absurdity, members of a generation much obsessed by death (witness the opening of *Man's Estate* or *The Outsider*), but responding to this sense of death not by turning to art (which was the solution of Proust, Joyce, and their generation), but by concentrating on life with all its death and violence in a determination to extract from that condition an ideal by which to live. This ideal is achieved by a hero of a particular kind: the picaresque saint – a saint with more than a touch of the rogue about him: 'It is exactly in their impurity – whether it is reckoned by official morality or by any other kind – that the saintly characters achieve, and in fact incarnate, that trust in life and that companionship that the contemporary novel so emphasizes. They are outsiders who share; they are outcasts who enter in' (Lewis, p. 33).

In following this pattern, whereby a hero is created and a value achieved, Lewis moves from Camus who indicates a positive revolt to the quasi-religious Faulkner and finally to Graham Greene whose world still exhibits the horror, the boredom, but also the glory. It was in the preface to the French edition of *The Power and the Glory* that Mauriac described that novel as the answer to the widespread sense of Absurdity.

Lewis's choice of novelists is international: Malraux and Camus are French, Moravia and Silone Italian, Faulkner American, and Greene English. From their work he traces the gradual emergence of an ambiguous hero, and the value of companionship with religious overtones as a response to Absurdity. A similar pattern emerges from Ihab Hassan's study of the contemporary novel, *Radical Innocence* (1961), but Hassan is exclusively concerned with American novelists, and by 'contemporary' he means the generation writing *after* the Second World War. Hassan suggests that a literate Martian looking at our bookshelves full of contemporary novels would conclude that the planet Earth was on the way to self-destruction, and that the present world is such that man lives under the constant threat of death, and can only respond by being rebel or victim. The hero, therefore, must be a confused and mixed character – a mixture of saint and criminal – whose innocence is met by the destructive nature of his experience, and who finds himself in a truly existential situation. In his first chapter Hassan describes this existential situation in some detail, pointing out that America and Europe share the same experience and respond in a combination of Prometheus and Sisyphus: the eternal rebel and the eternal victim (Hassan, pp. 31–2).

By this time, however, novelists are no longer concerned with Absurdity, which they take for granted, but only with the consequences: Hassan's résumé has the matter-of-fact tone of historical description. And, if America shares European experience of Absurdity, she brings to it her own particular tradition which is already a clash between hope and despair, arising historically from the enormous expectations of American society and their failure to materialize. American literature is full of young and innocent characters whose confrontation with experience is painful and, in some cases, fatal. Existential Man, therefore, with his crisis, is not very far from the hero who already exists in American literature.

Chance and absurdity rule human action, and this the hero recognizes, knowing that reality is another name for chaos. Consequently there are no accepted norms of feeling or conduct, and, therefore, courage is the prime virtue because it implies self-sufficiency. Whether rebel or victim, the hero is at odds with society, his motives are forever mixed, his perception of the situation remains limited and relative, and his actions cut across the lines conventionally drawn between good and evil. To deal with this as objectively as possible, the novelist chooses a highly organized form and relies on universal symbols and, in a highly technical discussion of particular authors and their forms, Hassan comes to the general conclusion that the solution is irony, and a blurring of the distinction usually held between tragedy and comedy (Hassan, pp. 116 ff.).

The choice of irony seems almost inevitable because of the double nature of this kind of utterance. Basically, dramatic irony in Greek drama meant that the audience, aware of the facts of the play, understood from the words spoken by characters unaware of their own future more than the words, in their immediate sense, implied. The contemporary hero shares with Oedipus, for example, an ignorance of his situation which the audience, alive to the Absurd situation, sees only too clearly. But irony can also commit itself to that which it criticizes and it is therefore suitable as a mediator between what Hassan describes as 'the hero's outrageous dream and the sadness of human mortality' (Hassan, pp. 329–30).

Where Hassan illustrates the response to Absurdity in thirteen novelists, David Galloway chooses only four in his *The Absurd*

Hero in American Fiction (1966). He points out (citing Camus) that the novel is an ideal form for mirroring the confrontation of intention and reality, but the concept as laid down in *The Myth of Sisyphus* will differ in the novel from its use in the theatre, as described by Esslin, because the surfaces of a novel are more conventionally 'realistic' than those in the plays of Ionesco and Beckett. Galloway's criticism is different in another important way, for he has chosen deliberately what he calls four examples (Updike, Styron, Saul Bellow, and J. D. Salinger) of *optimistic* chroniclers of the Absurd, who share a belief that man can establish values in an Absurdist world. The epithetic 'optimistic' fits awkwardly on the noun Absurdity, but Galloway believes that these writers suggest paths through the modern Wasteland, and they do so by accepting Absurdity and exploring the consequences. *The Myth of Sisyphus* is discussed not because Camus was an influence, but because that essay still offers the analysis and terminology of our modern environment, with its vision of spiritual sterility and loneliness shared by these contemporary American writers. Recognizing that demands for order make man absurd, and, like Camus, rejecting both orthodoxy and nihilism, their rebellious hero hopes to create values which will replace the lost ones. And their solution is another variant of companionship, love:

> These heroes all begin their quests with a vision of the apparent lack of meaning in the world, of the mendacity and failure of ideals, but they conclude with gestures of affirmation derived explicitly from their realization of the significance of love.
>
> (Galloway, p. 171)

This value reaffirms belief in human beings as such, and goes beyond the Absurd. If, like Camus, such writers as Bellow and Salinger see the universe as walls closing round a diminishing hero, they conclude, nevertheless, that only individual will and responsibility, the sincere private gesture, can make this position tenable, an attitude upheld, Galloway finds, by irony – an irony which, once more, is not a reflection of nihilism, and which we can best understand by reference to Absurdity rather than account for by Absurdity.

Several impressions emerge. Firstly, the novel, like drama and philosophy, arrives at a platitude: love and the ironic method. The progress of contemporary American novelists is remarkably similar to that of Malraux with one exception: they do not have to define Absurdity, merely accept it as their *donnée*. This is inevitable; as with drama, one or two Absurd novels more or less exhaust the subject, and subsequent artists who grow up in an environment where Absurdity is already defined move to solutions for a meaningless world, most of which look suspiciously like 'leaps of faith'. For critics the term, as in drama, has become a useful shorthand by which they 'explain' contemporary literature. Noticeably there is a loss of the anguish which characterized the early novels, for anguish and platitudes do not go well together. By 1960, however, Absurdity was nearly forty years old. The surprising thing is that the intense period in the drama does not occur until 1950, but it must be remembered that the theatre is slow to adapt because its audience is a mass. Ironically, it is this belated intensity which has done most to bring Absurdity into prominence, and produced its richest expression: which is why, in the last analysis, Esslin's appropriation of the term was both right and fortunate.

11

Conclusion

John Russell Taylor concludes his entry on Absurd Theatre by saying that it had spent its force by 1962, and Charles Marowitz, in the same year (1966) agreed ('British Theatre', *Tulane Drama Review*, No. 34, 1966, pp. 203–6. The whole issue is very helpful.) An end to Absurdity should come as no surprise: we cannot live permanently in an extreme situation, and that 'ferocious hopefulness' of which Camus accused the philosophers is a basic instinct, and one, moreover, not without rational support. Once we have got over the shock, common sense tells us that the shock is self-destructive. But whereas Marowitz speaks scornfully of 'a brief vogue labelled Theatre of the Absurd', and 'absurd' as a synonym for potty and screwed-up, Taylor points out that its effects as 'a liberating influence on conventional theatre' continue. Absurd drama in its short career *has* liberated. Sartre's concept of freedom leading to revolt is, whatever its consequences, liberation. Herbert Blau in 1954 wrote that if nausea, angst, fear, and trembling are the stock-in-trade of Absurd drama, that drama was fundamentally 'liberating' and the plays have shown 'intelligence, novelty and charm' – qualities sadly lacking in contemporary theatre. (*The Impossible Theatre*, pp. 256 and 307).

What they have liberated is energy of the kind Wilson Knight has called Dionysian. Ostensibly writing about Kitchen Sink plays, Wilson Knight cut across the artificial boundaries between Anger and Absurdity to suggest that in our time literature draws its numinous impact not from ghosts or demons, but from material objects and human inventions:

The complications of a materialistic civilization, in all their constricting paradox and metaphysical inadequacy, make our terror. Today ghosts, or any intimation of some less clogged order of being, are likely to bring fresh air and sanity. That is the point at which we have arrived.

(*Encounter*, December 1963, Vol. XXI, No. 6, pp. 48–54)

Absurd fiction has lost its anguish, and the term has become historical. It can indeed be applied contemptuously as was 'metaphysical' to a certain kind of poetry. But to call John Donne's 'Nocturnall upon St. Lucies Day' metaphysical is useful and accurate; in a similar fashion *Waiting for Godot* is Absurd not absurd. If Absurdity has a moral it is for us to discover it.

Select Bibliography

In producing this bibliography, as in writing the monograph, I have given preference to works of good quality that are readily available; many of them have large and excellent bibliographies to guide the reader in further reading.

The indispensable work is, of course, MARTIN ESSLIN, *The Theatre of the Absurd*, Penguin, revised and enlarged, 1968, with an excellent bibliography, but JOHN RUSSELL TAYLOR'S *Anger and After*, London, 1962, revised 1969, is both comprehensive and useful.

In the particular field of French drama DAVID I. GROSSVOGEL, *The Self-Conscious Stage in Modern French Drama*, New York, 1958, published as *Twentieth Century French Drama*, 1961, prepares the way for Esslin's treatment. Extremely useful, with bibliography and appendices, is JACQUES GUICHARNAUD (with JUNE BECKELMAN), *Modern French Theatre*, New Haven, 1961; also L. C. PRONKO, *Avant-Garde*, University of California Press, 1962, and, because it concerns itself with Protest as well as Absurdity, G. E. WELLWARTH, *The Theater of Protest and Paradox*, New York, 1964. Useful material can be found in ROGER SHATTUCK, *The Banquet Years*, London, 1959.

RAYMOND WILLIAMS, *Modern Tragedy*, London, 1966, discusses 'tragedy' leading to modern examples including Ionesco, Sartre, Beckett, and Camus; and J. L. STYAN, *The Dark Comedy*, Cambridge, 1962, revised 1968, is a useful history of the development of contemporary tragi-comedy.

I consider the work of ERIC BENTLEY absolutely vital: *The*

Life of the Drama, London, 1965, usefully studies the basic terms of drama, and *The Playwright as Thinker*, Cleveland, Ohio, 1946, published in England as *The Modern Theatre: A Study of Dramatists and the Drama*, 1948, is immensely rich in illustration and perception, with excellent bibliographical material. The reader may also find his anthology of documents, modestly described as 'a bundle of hints', useful: *The Theory of the Modern Stage*, Penguin, 1968.

COLIN WILSON's anthology *The Outsider*, London, 1956, is stimulating.

On Malraux, W. M. FROHOCK, *André Malraux and the Tragic Imagination*, Stanford, 1952, is a helpful introduction. On Camus, JOHN CRUICKSHANK provides a full treatment of both philosophy and literature in *Albert Camus and the Literature of Revolt*, London, 1959; the novels and the two plays are published by Penguin. The philosophy of Jean-Paul Sartre is lucidly explained by MARY WARNOCK in *The Philosophy of Sartre*, London, 1966, and PHILIP THODY's *Jean-Paul Sartre*, London, 1961, complements this with a discussion of the literature. To these I would add IRIS MURDOCH's *Sartre*, London, 1953. *Nausea* and the plays are published by Penguin. L. C. PRONKO's pamphlet *Eugène Ionesco*, Columbia University Press, 1965, is brief and readable, but R. N. COE's *Ionesco*, Edinburgh, 1961, remains indispensable. R. N. COE's *Beckett*, Edinburgh, 1964, in the same 'Writers and Critics Series' could be complemented by F. J. HOFFMAN's study *Samuel Beckett: The Language of Self*, New York, 1964, and R. N. COE's *The Vision of Jean Genet*, London, 1968, by the more literary treatment provided by PHILIP THODY in *Jean Genet*, London, 1968. Harold Pinter is considered in ARNOLD P. HINCHLIFFE's *Harold Pinter*, New York, 1967. A Christian interpretation can be found in J. CHIARI, *Landmarks of Contemporary Drama*, London, 1965. C. W. E. Bigsby's study of *Albee* is welcome, Edinburgh, 1969.

On the novelists the works cited are:

JOHN KILLINGER, *Hemingway and the Dead Gods*, Kentucky, 1960.

R. W. B. LEWIS, *The Picaresque Saint*, London, 1960 – with an excellent chapter on Camus.

IHAB HASSAN, *Radical Innocence*, Princeton, 1961.

DAVID GALLOWAY, *The Absurd Hero in American Fiction*, Austin, Texas, 1966.

The following collections of essays are often helpful:

The Encore Reader, ed. Marowitz, Milne and Hale, London, 1965.

Modern British Dramatists, ed. J. R. Brown, Twentieth Century Views, Englewood Cliffs, N.J., 1968.

Modern American Theatre, ed. A. B. Kernan, Twentieth Century Views, 1967.

Samuel Beckett, ed. Martin Esslin, Twentieth Century Views, 1965.

Theatre in the Twentieth Century, ed. R. W. Corrigan, New York, 1963.

Contemporary Theatre, Stratford-upon-Avon Studies No. 4, London, 1962.

American Theatre, Stratford-upon-Avon Studies No. 10, London, 1967.

Aspects of Drama and the Theatre, Sydney, 1965.

'British Theatre', *Tulane Drama Review*, Vol. 11 (No. 2) T 34 (Winter, 1966), is a lively survey of ten years in that institution.

Index